# COLOSSIANS

Read it all, but these scriptures has the Holy Spirit put in my heart mightily.

1: 10 - 17, 22, 27-29
2: 1 - 10
3: 10 -14, 23-25
4: 3 - 5

"That their hearts might be comforted, being knit together in love, and unto all riches of the full assurance of understanding, to the acknowledgement of the mystery of God, and of the Father, and of Christ; In whom are hid all the treasures of wisdom and knowledge."

2: 2-3

# Seventh Messenger

Frederick F. Haussman Jr.

ISBN 978-1-64458-188-9 (paperback)
ISBN 978-1-64458-189-6 (digital)

Christian Faith Publishing, Inc.
832 Park Avenue
Meadville, PA 16335
www.christianfaithpublishing.com

Printed in the United States of America

"Angels are spirits, but it is not because they are spirits that they are angels. They become Angels when they are sent For the name Angel refers to their office, not their nature. You ask the name of this nature. It is spirit; you ask its office. It is that of an angel, which is a messenger." (St. Augustine, 354–430 CE)

The word *angel* comes from ancient Greek word *angelos*, meaning "messenger." *Angelos* were the translation of a Hebrew word *mal-ak*, which also means "messenger." So as St. Thomas Aquinas pointed out in his great theological work *Summa Theologiae* (1266–1273), "We define, and can only define, angels by what they do, and not by what they are."

They are messengers.

# Congratulations!

God owns the rainbow.
You're buying the right book.

If you know for sure something terrible is going to happen to the earth, would you tell the people of the world, even though they might not believe you but despise you, even hate you or want to kill you?

"These things I command you, that you love one another. If the world hates you, you know that it hated me before it hated you. If you are of the world, the world would love its own: but because you are not of the world, but I have chosen you out of the world, therefore the world hats you" (John 15:17–19).

Would you tell them? God is telling me to tell you.

Please keep this in mind this book is short because you do not need to know all of Freddy's life. You need to know the Father, Son, and Holy Spirit, and how real they are for your soul! It's your soul that goes on to be with the Father. You need to read the Father's words in the Holy Bible. Let his words speak to you through the Holy Spirit. Let his love fill you just like he does all his children and Freddy in a big way!

There is only one way to the Tree of Life— that is, you must accept the Christ of the Father, named Yasha, or Jesus!

May the love of the Father fill you through his Holy Spirit to the truth in Christ Jesus. Amen.

Take away all the words written in black in this book, and what is left is all you need. Words in purple are wisdom and truth.

"The world is a great mirror, it reflects back to you what you are. If you are loving, if you are friendly, if you are helpful the world will prove loving and friendly and helpful to you, the world is what You are." (Thomas Dreier; read 1st John 4:16–17 and 1st Corinthians 13:1– 13 and James 1:22–27.)

"It's all coming true, and it's all being witness now by you."

# Foreword

I'm ready to tell my secret; it's written to let the people on the earth know how the Father of us all, his Son, and his Holy Spirit gives me loving-kindness. I have been on this road of life, fighting from telling people who I am in Christ Jesus—that is, I'm the seventh angel, the messenger as described in Revelation 10. "I swear by Him who lives for ever and ever, who created heaven, and the things that are they're in, and the earth, and the things they're in, and the sea, and the things they're in, that there should be time no longer" (Revelation 10:6).

Time no longer means it will be too late for your name to be added to the Lamb's book of life, to be believers in Christ, for it will be closed. I will cry with a loud voice, and the seven thunders will utter their voices. Soon after, in God's timing, the whole earth will shake violently and it will. "Blessed are they which are

called unto the marriage supper of the Lamb"
(Revelation 19:9).

Except Yasha, Jesus, the Christ of the Father,
before the whole earth shakes. The seven thunders will have uttered their voices in this book,
which from before the foundation of the world,
God has given to me to tell the people of earth;
because the world will have a great earth-shak-
ing movement (Isaiah 13:13, Ezekiel 33:1–11,
and Revelation 16:17–18).

If you do not believe that Yasha, Jesus, is the
Christ of God (God came to earth in human
form), then your name is not in the Lamb's
book of life. Your name is not on the guest list
of the marriage supper of the Lamb. "Many are
called, but few are chosen." Christ blood shied,
forgives you and me of our sins, his Holy Spirit
comes into our heart and mind, the Christ of
God, who died on the cross, for all people sins
past, present, future, then the Father who has
risen his Christ, lets his Holy Spirit fill your
whole body with joys unspeakable, heavenly
love. Believe that Jesus is the Christ of the
Father, Creator of all, and then your name will

be added to the Lamb's book of life; his love is so wonderful. I will put into my words my life story. I have sinned a lot, and yet his arms are still stretched out. You reading this, time is running out. Make sure that your name is in the Lamb's book of life now, because when the whole earth shakes, it means the Lamb's book of life is closed. In Revelation 16:17–18 reads, "It is done." Then the whole earth shakes, and life on earth will be harder until Christ returns, and the New Jerusalem comes down to the new earth. I'm not sure when that happens. I only know the big earthquake is coming. Read on about how the Father, our Creator, revealed it all to me, how great his loving-kindness is. Pray you have ears to hear and eyes to see. May God open your heart and mind to the truth. What the Father has for your soul for not believing in Christ, whose name is Yasha, Jesus the Christ of God our heavenly Father, I can't even put down on paper, but the Bible says, "For it is a shame to even speak of those things which are done to them in secret" (Ephesians 5:12).

# Miracles by the Father, Son, and Holy Spirit

Chapter 1

1. At ten months old, he heard the voice mind, and eyes were opened.
2. At five years old, he was bit by scorpion, and an angel carried him home.

Chapter 3

3. Prayer to get out of Philly at eleven years old.
4. At twelve years old, he was baptized, and he felt the power of love so strong, and it was like the bubble of love surrounding Freddy.
5. At sixteen, the Holy Spirit told Freddy to be a preacher!

6. In the year 1971, he started trying to read the Bible, and his eyes were wide open. He felt enlightened, and his dyslexia was gone!

## Chapter 4

7. At twenty-three, he was enlightened, and his third eye was opened. He started his spiritual walk from Fort Lauderdale to Daytona Beach.

8. On the seventh day, he experienced the *love* of the Holy Spirit that was more powerful than what he felt after being baptized. He was back from the walk, lost his love, and found real love.

9. He went into a 40-day fast and camped in the woods. He read the Word and gained wisdom from the Father regarding the seven thunders that will utter their voices.

## Chapter 5

10. After an exhausting day at work, God touched him while lying facedown in bed.

11. He took the road to earthly love for a girl.

12. He got ripped off for three hundred pounds of pot. He read the big Bible and was given the bullet that was for death.

13. In 1978, he got busted with two thousand pounds of pot. The Father opened Freddy's heart again to follow him.

14. In 1978, he was on trial and saved by God again by being sent to Eglin.

## Chapter 6

15. In 1980, he was back to the world ran by the rat race. But with three daughters, he still felt blessed.

16. In 1982, he was in a construction accident, but he was saved by the hands of God!

17.    In 1988, the orange tree that was dead came back to life with fruit in three days.

## Chapter 7

18.    In 1997, the Holy Spirit reassured Freddy he is the seventh angel, a messenger. He started to get things ready to make his website, www.seventhmessenger.com, go live.

19.    In 1998, the Holy Spirit said, "Your Bible will be stolen tonight!" He saved the little book, but he lost his Bible. It was a very sad day.

20.    In 1997, he set up the Seventh Messenger (Angel) website, and fear set in.

21.    He received financial blessing in Port Saint Lucie.

22.    In 2003, the Father showed him the New Jerusalem.

23.    In 2013, the Holy Spirit told him, "I have a better view for you!"

24.     In 2017, this is my story. These are the thunders that must utter their voices.

"It's time to roar! It is done!"

# Chapter 1

## Days of Future Past

> Time seems to stand quite still.
> In a child's world, it always will.
>                        —The Moody Blues

Freddy's great-grandfather and great-grand-mother on his dad's side moved to America years before World War I. They were of German descent, and their only child, a son, came with them. He was in his late teens. After living in America for years, the son married an Irish girl. She was born in America, and her family arrived in 1849. As the World War 1 started, their son, Frederick, was born in America. "God bless America, land that I love. Stand beside her and guide her with the light that shines from above.

From the mountains to the valleys to the ocean white with foam, God blessed America my home sweet home."

Frederick was two when his father died. His mother gave her baby boy to his German grandmother. His dad died, and his mother stepped out of his life, and she left with Frederick only sister. From two years old till his grandmother's death, he lived in the same house. He was sixteen when the people living in his grandmother's house kicked Frederick out after her funeral, and he was on the streets and out of school, with no one to turn to. His mother was out of the picture. His dreams were crushed! No one knows what he did to get by on the streets of Philly. He never talked about his teenage years.

Japan bombed Pearl Harbor, and World War II started. Frederick was twenty-three. Then he was employed as a member of the armed forces. He knew how to speak and understood German, so off he went to save the world from Hitler and his own race. Hitler and his people became vain in their imagination, and their foolish hearts were darkened. Professing to be wise, they became dead fools! The fool has said in his heart, there is no God (Psalm 53:1, KJV)!

The young twenty-seven-year-old man was one of the blessed ones. He got back from World War II with only a wound in his left arm. He never talked about the war or his youth, but he received some medals during his time in the army, and he took some of them from dead Germans. He had some pictures of him and his buddies standing in front of tents and jeeps and around foxholes. Some of them were with prisoners. If it were not for the uniforms, we looked like brothers. We all bleed red when are cut. Right! Whether you believe it or not, we are all God's children, hallelujah! We are loved with a special kind of love.

With a movie-star look—tall, dark, and handsome, with superblue eyes and a great smile. He dabbled in the modeling industry but did not like the phony side of the business, especially kissing up to people to get the job. Maybe it was the new gal who came into his life. He glided into sales with his showbiz state of mind.

The attractive young woman came into his life two years after the war was over. She was seven years younger, a hairstylist who had her own shop with one of her sisters. She was five feet four, and slim with long dark hair, a lovely smile, a beautiful nose, and green eyes with a small gold spot in the left corner of the right eye. Her family arrived in the late 1700s, who were of Irish and English descent, with a little Native American blood. She was the seventh out of nine children born to a housewife and dad who was a union plumber at her birth. Her dad started his own business as she got older. His shop was in the basement of their home. She was born and raised in Philly, just like her parents, and their parents. The young woman was deeply in love with the handsome man who just got back from the war. They did what all young lovers do, fell deeply in love and loved being with each other.

Love, to my
sweetheart

Love is substance! Lust and illusion,
Only in the surge of passion
Do they mingle in confusion.

They married and then bought a house in the small town outside of Philadelphia, named Ivyland, a two-story house with a white picket fence around the front yard. Ten months later, the first child was born, and she was a beautiful blue-eyed girl. This was a piece of cake for the newlyweds. Having one child is easy on them both; her mother came from a family of nine.

The second child was born to the attractive couple in the year 1949, the first boy. They named him after his dad, Frederick, but they called him Freddy, born in the land of brotherly love. His name means "peaceful ruler." Seven times seven is forty-nine.

"But when it pleased God, who separated me from my mother's womb, and called me by his grace, to reveal his Son in me, that I might preach him among the heathen" (Galatians 1:15–16).

"And thou shalt number seven Sabbaths of years unto thee, seven times seven years; and the space of the seven Sabbaths of years shall be unto thee forty and nine years. Then shalt thou cause the trumpet of the jubilee to sound on the tenth day of the seventh month, in the Day of Atonement shall you make the trumpet sound throughout all your land" (Leviticus 25:8–9).

Truly, truly, I say unto you little Freddy is around ten months old. He is in the crib sitting up. He's looking up at a figure. He is watching and not really understanding what's going on. His mind is in baby land, seeing but not understanding.

What's happening is, Daddy's entertaining the boy, who is sitting up watching. His back is up against the back of the crib, with the wall behind him. The baby boy is watching this finger and then the voice on the inside of his mind whispering in his right ear. It is a deep voice, yet the whisper is soft. "He's tricking you!" And, again, he hears, "He's tricking you!" As soon as the voice stops, Freddy's mind is open! He sees this man. He feels as though he is a young boy with understanding. He knows he is in a body of a baby that can't talk. He sees what the person is doing. His mind is open to understanding, and the dad is pretending to put these little glass animals in his mouth, and then they appear out of his ear. He's doing it over and over. He's tricking him. He sees it and understands it as clear as day. He couldn't talk. He could not tell Daddy about how he is tricking him, how he sees him, or about the voice; but he sees and knows he's being tricked. The voice opens his mind to understanding. After seeing just enough of the trick, the enlightenment is gone, and he is just a baby again. The only thing that stands out in his mind is the picture, what happened that day, how he saw his dad, and that voice that opened his mind for a moment of time. This is burned into his subconscious mind. At separate stages in his life, when he needs to hear of things that will happen to him and this world, the voice comes.

"And when he shall begin to sound, the mystery of God, it is finished, as he has declared to his servants the prophets" (Revelation 10:7).

A year goes by. The parents have another beautiful girl who has the look of her mother.

Mother sells her portion of the hair shop to her sister. There are three children now. Mother is a stay-at-home wife and stayed that way for the next twenty years. Once a month, she takes the trolley car to see her mother with all three children. She is a strong but very loving mother.

Dad is working harder now, bringing home the bacon. It is not as easy now with three children. Dad is so good in sales; he is given a new position, but he must move the family to the great state of Texas.

They move, and the family lives twenty miles outside the city of Dallas. The young lad is growing up in a white house with a big front yard; a backyard with lots of shade trees; and a bigger backyard that was fenced in, where they had goats, sheep, chickens, ducks, and a barn with one beautiful grayish-white horse with a white mane and tail. It is Dad who bought the farm. Here's the father and mother living in the great state of Texas. They grew up in the big dirty city, and they have no clue about raising animals like these, but they are trying to make it all work, especially with three kids. It is the year 1953, and the kids are happy. Mother is happy, helpful, and a good cook. There is peace, love, and happiness in the home. The family is flying back to the land of brotherly love. Mother buys her little four-year-old son a pair of cowboy boots. He wears them on his first airplane ride back to Philly. He's going to see Grandmom and Grandpop, aunts, and uncles on his mother's side and their children. His dad would like to find his mother to see if she is still living. Only through pictures does the young lad remember the trip, but the picture and voice of the Holy Spirit when he spoke to him remains tattooed in his consciousness; he knew then it was the time his mind became open to understanding. He never told anyone about this enlightening experience until now.

Two years go by quickly. Mother is pregnant, and nine months later, another girl is born. Back home in Texas, they would go to church every Sunday for four years now in a Baptist church, as most families did in the fifties. Mom and Dad set a good example through their actions. The whole family goes to church, and this triggers

the young lad's hunger and thirst for a relationship with his heavenly Father, who has opened
his heart and mind back in the land of brotherly
love.

> For thou have possessed my reins:
> thou has covered me in my moth-
> er's womb. I will praise you; for
> I am fearfully and wonderfully
> made: marvelous are your works;
> and that my soul knows right well.
> My substance was not hid from
> you, when I was made in secret,
> and curiously wrought in the low-
> est parts of the earth. Your eyes
> did see my substance, yet being
> unperfected; and in your book,
> all my members were written,
> which in continuance were fash-
> ioned, when as yet there was none
> of them. How precious also are
> your thoughts unto me, O God!
> How great is the sum of them!
> (Psalm 139:13)

The young lad learns this prayer when he is four years old from his mother: "Now I lay me down to sleep, I pray the Lord my soul to keep. If I should die before I wake, I pray the Lord my soul to take."

But in his little mind, he thinks, what is a soul?

The young lad would say this prayer every night while he is on his knees at the side of his bed in his own room. He adds, "God bless Mommy, Daddy, and my sisters." He adds, "When do I get a brother to play with?"

In his mind, he keeps wondering what a soul is, but he never asks anyone about it: What is a soul? The boy believed in God with his whole heart and mind. He feels the presence of God's Spirit within him, and he knows he is. How he loves praying to the Father. He feels an unspeakable joy whenever he thinks of his heavenly Father. He is a child now in love with God. It's easier when you're world is small. He has no clue about Jesus the Christ of God or the Holy Spirit, the voice of God. Just God, that's all!

"But for us also, to whom it shall be imputed, if we believe on him, that raised up Jesus our Lord from the dead; who was delivered for our offences, and was raised again for our justification" (Romans 4:24–25).

"Through the eyes of a child you will come out to see. That your world is spinning around and through life you will be a small part of a hope of a love that excise, through the eyes of a child you will see" (The Moody Blues, *To Our Children's Children's Children*).

As the young lad grows, he loves jumping off the top of the barn, where the horse lives. The bottom part is made of wood; from the top of the roof to the ground was about eight feet. The roof is metal; it slopes down to five feet where he could stand on the edge. He believes he is an angel, and can fly. He jumps off the edge of the barn and quickly lands on the ground, and he feels what seems like lighting running through his veins. He climbs up the tree that stands next to the barn, gets on the roof, slides down to the edge, and jumps again, landing on his feet. The young lad has lots of fun in his little cowboy world.

He loves music and listens to newly released rock and roll songs. His parents like music. The family car has a radio, plus another one in the living room. In the garage, he plays Elvis's first hit song, "You Ain't Nothin' but a Hound Dog," on his big sister's small 45 record player.

He can't let his big sister know he does this. It's only when she over a friend's house. He's almost six and can't wait till he starts school. Big sister is already in the second grade, and she is smart and loves school. She's very pretty and has lots of friends. All the girls and boys like her. When school starts, he is told by his mother he must wait till next year to start school. He has to be six by the start of school; he'd miss it by a month. There is no preschool.

Then came one day, on the roof of the barn, he jumped and he slipped on some leaves, and he landed on the ground on his belly. He got the air knocked out of him. He couldn't even cry. He had no breath of air. He couldn't call to his mommy, and if he could, he was told not to jump off the top of the barn! He did it more than he could count. He was lying on his back on the ground, with no air taken into or expelling from his lungs, a breath of air blown into his mouth down into his lungs. He blew it out, and he could breathe again! No broken bones, no cuts—he's okay. He stood up. He brushed the dirt off his shirt and pants. He didn't tell anyone; he kept it to himself, but he knew God had something to do with it. After that day, he stopped jumping off the barn. The thought of being an angel left his mind. He'd decided to keep his feet on solid ground from then on, and be a cowboy.

> Understanding is a well-spring of life unto him that has it. (Proverbs 16:22)

Dad bought the family's first black-and-white television set. In the mornings, after eating, he watched the *Captain Kangaroo* show, then the *Howdy Dundee* show, which got them glued to the TV.

He watched *The Long Ranger* after lunch. This classic radio show was brought to television in 1949 and was a favorite of children and adults alike. The young lad loved Clayton Moore as the masked man, Silver, his horse, and the faithful sidekick, Tonto. The story concerns a Texas ranger who is the only survivor of an ambush; his brother, Captain Reed, is one of the men who got killed. He is nursed back to health by his friend Tonto. Tonto tells the ranger after seeing a ring around his neck, "You are Kemosabe!" It means a "trusty scout." Tonto gave the ring to the ranger after he saved his life when they were young teenagers when the white man killed his Indian family. Years have gone by, and things are revered. After his recovery from his injuries, the ranger decides to dedicate his life to bring justice and peace to the West. Little Freddy's favorite show, The Lone Ranger, a cowboy's best friend, Kemosobe, a trusted scout.

*Superman* was also aired on TV before or sometimes just after dinner. After *Superman* was over, he would fly around the living room and beat up the long sofa pillows. Life in America was heaven in his young mind. They ate pretty much at the same time each day. Sometimes when Dad made it home from his many long weeks of sales trips, he always had a present for the kids. They loved Daddy.

The young lad had two best friends, Ronald and David-Mike. Ron lived farther away, and his parents were best friends of Freddy's mom and dad. David-Mike lived three houses down. Homes were far apart. They walked. He had no bike. David-Mike was a gifted artist. Freddy was amazed at how he could draw anything at his age. David-Mike was a good friend. His dad looked like Clark Kent, Superman, as a reporter. He wore the hat and his suit; he wore the black-rimmed glasses, white shirt, and tie. He was even built like him. For a year, the young lad thought he might even be Superman.

This was one of the coolest thing the boys would do when they got together. It was to go crawdad fishing. They would walk to the end of the street where the creek was. The creek water would slowly go through the tunnels that ran under the road after a good rain.

When the creek was low, they would go down the banks, where the water flowed over a cement slab; it must have been eighth to ten feet down to that slab. The boys could stand on the cement and put a piece of bacon on their hooks or bread, but bacon worked best. They would drop their line into the water, wait for the pull on the line, and catch a crawdad. They would pull them out of the water and lay them onto the cement. These crawdads are a cross between a scorpion and a lobster. The tails are like the lobsters, but the claws are that of the scorpion. You'd have to be fast to pick one up. You would use your thumb and finger and right behind the head, real fast! Grab them! To slow and your little fingers got pinched, Ouch! Many of times the boys got pinched. After looking at them, they just put them back in the water so they could catch them again the tug on the line was the thrill. They are living in a world of innocence. They would laugh at each other, having the bests of times being childlike. "Verily I say unto you, whosoever shall not receive the kingdom of God as a child shall in no wise enter therein" (Luke 18:17).

Freddy living the American dream, a wonderful childhood life, I'm talking about better then Leave it to Beaver, but that TV show did not happen till later. No school, all play, all day. The boys would take off on foot to all four corners of their little world and take a lunch if need be.

Some days, they just stopped at any given neighbor's house for some cookies and milk. Everyone knew each other and which kids were whose.

It's the weekend. Freddy already turned seven, and he was going to spend the night at David-Mike's house. A year earlier, Freddy took a nickel he found at David-Mike's house. When confronted by his dad on how he got the nickel, he said, "I found it at David-Mike's!"

"That's stealing, son!" Dad took the boy by the hand and walked him to David-Mike's house to hand the nickel to David-Mike's dad, "Superman," and said, "I'm sorry I took your nickel."

"A wise son hears his father's instruction" (Proverbs).

Freddy's dad was six feet three with big hands. He let the boy know that taking anything from anyone's home without asking is stealing. It was a good two days before the young lad could sit down, and he slept on his tummy. He knew stealing was bad. This is one of many real lessons learned in life from his dad.

Now back at the Friday night sleepover. The boys are in David-Mike's bedroom, and he is showing Freddy's drawings, cowboys around covered wagons with Indians in the background. He is amazed at his talent in drawing people, the boys being the same age. They talk about how cool it will be to make a covered wagon, with the help of his dad. Lights out, they dream in America, land of the free cowboys, home of the brave Indians.

Saturday morning, David-Mike's mother makes them a breakfast treat. In a tall clean glass, she puts a scoop of ice cream that drop to bottom of glass, then she put in Forested flakes some more ice cream then Cheerios then ice cream with rice crispes on top. The boys look with eyes wide open, licking their lips. It's so good they ask for another.

"Sorry, kids, one is enough for now." They leave the table and wait in the backyard till their dad is done with his eggs and ham, his coffee, and toast with raspberry jam, which one of the ladies in the neighborhood made. The boys are up for this, to build a small covered wagon using the old wood and an old wagon that David-Mike's dad had been saving just for this project. He is a dad who spends time with his son. Not too many dads did so back then. The morning is cool. The kids have on a coat running around, as the dad walks out to the big backyard. They had no animals at home, but there is a big shed for his lawn mower and tools. He tells the boys to get the wood that is stacked by the shed. Freddy does not see the camouflage scorpion as he is putting his right hand on the woodpile to pull one out with his left hand. As he grabs one piece of wood, the scorpion stings the top of his left hand.

He sees him walk away. You know how they have that walk of theirs, with their tail up in the air and little legs carrying that flat body, with the big claws just like the crawdads. You talk about pain! The hand blows up like a balloon; the burning, stinging, pulsating never-ending pain was getting worse every second, crying his eyes out as he is being carried all the way home by David- Mike's dad. Mama put some lotion that is kept in the bathroom and wraps his hand with bandages. He is put to bed, crying himself to sleep.

Sometime in the evening, as the sun was setting, he was dreaming. There were three very pretty, young girls; each of them looked different. They had an assorted-color glow about them. They came floating in the air to the boy after he had fallen off the seesaw in the park and hurt his head. They told him, "You'll be all right, my child." When they picked him up, he'd stop crying, and they carried the boy as they floated in the air. The dream felt so real. This couldn't be a dream. Then putting him in his mother's arms, they said he would be all right. The next morning, Freddy woke up to a healed hand. He believed that angels healed him, but at seven, he thought that's how it worked believing in God. Everyone knew this! He is with us if we believe. God does the healing. We are his children. "Through the eyes of a child you will see" (Moody Blues).

He played with friends, and Mother was making breakfast, lunch, and dinner; the young lad was watching the TV, as there was no preschool. Freddy and his friends played lots of baseball, did fishing, and exploring all around the new homes being built a few streets over, the big pipes being put in the ground for water runoff. A short man could stand up and walk through the tunnels. The boys went farther each day through the dark tunnels, using their imagination fighting different evil forces on any given day, the love of the unknown, and playing with buddies.

Summer was over, and not more than two weeks since the start of school, the young lad had his first encounter with love for a girl. Before he started school, the only girls he knew were his big sister and two younger sisters he has only been on this plant seven years.

This puppy love, what a thrill! It's like lighting running through your veins. This thrill is better than jumping off the barn, when you look at a girl, and your heart skips a beat. Freddy was hook on that puppy love. School was fun but difficult; no one knew what dyslexia was in 1956. We know now it's a disorder involving difficulty in learning to read or interpret words, letters, and other symbols.

This would haunt him from first grade through twelfth grade, since he would have a very hard time reading and remembering what he read. This was the case until he was twenty-one, when his mind was opened, and dyslexia left his mind. God's wisdom came in. His wisdom was his new love.

Freddy's buddy Ron's grandmother lived outside the area of their town, in a very old white three-story house. It stood alone. There was no other house around the area as far as the eye could see. She had a big pool in the yard, with trees all around the house. Over the years, they would go over to swim. Ron had a lot of relatives and friends who would use this pool. The young lad didn't know this, but they were Jehovah Witnesses. One beautiful summer weekend, the boys are in the pool having lots of fun, and other families were there. After swimming for about an hour, two older boys swam over to the young Freddy. He was by himself, with his arm on the side of the pool. He knew who they were. He said hi. One held him, and the other went under the water, pulled down his swim pants, and sucked on his private part. It's over quick. They swam away laughing. The lad was frightened. He didn't know how he would tell someone. They were young teenagers whom he knew could hurt him. He was afraid. It never happened again.

"It is a strange picture of men given over to unbelief and sin, and who see not, because they reject the true light" (Aristotle).

"The dominion sin has over you! Is according to the delight you have in it" (Psalms 19:13, John 8:34, Romans 6:13-15).

"'I found Israel like grapes in the wilderness. I saw your fathers as the first ripe in the fig tree at her first time: But they went to other gods, and separated themselves into that shame, and their abominations were according as they loved'" (Hosea 9:10).

"'Sometimes free will gets in the way, and man goes amiss. When men lay together in lust, it is surrender to the passions, and does nothing for the excellence in us'" (Aristotle).

"If wise men were hairs! The world would need a wig" (Austin O Malky).

Sin is in this world for now. We know in the Word of God, sex is between a man and a woman in the marriage bed. The pleasure in sex is something all humans can enjoy. If you're a male with a mind of a female or a female with a mind of a male, what would you do for love? There are all kinds of pleasure we could call sin. The Bible calls it sin if an unmarried man and a woman lives together! Kids having hook-ups, sin. How deep is your love for God, our Creator? It's so hurts the heart of the Father when you harm a child. Free will! Can you control your lust?

"'But whoso shall offend one of these little ones which believe in me, it were better for him that a millstone were hanged about his neck, and that he were drowned in the depth of the sea'" (Matthew 18:6).

Freddy's dad was gone a lot, sometimes weeks on end, all around the state. There were times the dad would take the boy to the pool where the colleges would compete. There were three levels of diving boards. His dad picked the highest levels in the diving area. Freddy would climb up to the very last level. The climb was scary itself, as well as the walk to the end of the board to dive off headfirst! It was high for anyone, let alone a little boy. His dad would be in the middle of the pool treading water, egging him on, "Come on, son, dive!" He was there to help him swim to the side of the pool. The boy was looking down; his daddy looked so small in the water. His short arms were not long enough to break the water before his head would hit the water. Falling so fast headfirst is like hitting a thick glass plate, and it hurts but then it turned into liquid. The head still hurts for another few minutes after you hit that water from that height, but the lad would dive headfirst over an over so he could spend time with his dad. He loved his daddy and saw him so little. That was the last time he spent quality time with dad. He was all ways making money for the family to live. By the Spirit of God, Freddy got even closer with God, and his love for God grew stronger, and he prayed every night on his knees beside his bed to thank his heavenly Father. "Thy kingdom come thy will be done on earth as it is in heaven."

# Chapter 2

### In Search of the Lost Cord

"This garden universe vibrates completely,
so we get a sound so sweet. Vibrations
reach on up to become light, then
through gamma out of sight"
(Moody Blues).

School was over; so did living in Texas. Dad left weeks in advance by car to have a house ready for the family to live in when they arrived. The movers packed all the things fast. With Dad gone, Mother took care of the three kids and a baby. Some of the items they packed went missing when they arrived in California. The movers were off to the highway. Mother and the kids all took a cab to the train station bound for

California. The entire day was spent just looking out the window at the unknown world passing him by; the best part of the train ride was
that they had their own sleeping cabin.

The family landed on the beaches of San
Diego. The house was on the beach when you
go out the front door the ocean air would enter
your nose filling your lungs with fresh sea air.
When you walk out onto the front wooden
porch, there were two layback wooden chairs
with cushions. Then you would walk down two
steps onto a round stepping stone walking on
to five of them. Then walk over to the white
wooden gate that open onto one long cement
pathway that was twelve feet wide, and the other
side the wall over two-foot-high, after the wall
was the white sandy beach, seeing the big blue
ocean with waves he never saw before coming in
with power, what a first-time picture for a little
boy.

The twelve-foot cemented walkway stretched
for miles and miles and miles along the beach.
Some houses were bigger than others, but they
were all facing the Pacific Ocean. Most days, the

young lad would walk to the seawall jump over onto the soft white sand, the ocean one hundred yards farther with big waves. He would play on the beach that summer—digging holes, making forts for his army men, or just walking up and down the beach, finding sand dollars and all kinds of shells or odd things that washed up from the mighty ocean. When sitting in the living room or on the front porch, you would witness a masterpiece, the hand of God putting together the breathtaking sunsets. Breathing in the beauty of living on the beach is heaven. This took his mind off Texas and the hunting trips he never got to go on and his two best friends. He didn't think of writing because of his dyslexia; he couldn't even read a comic book.

When the lad started fourth grade, the family stopped going to church. At school, he became friends with a boy his age, Justin. He was an inch taller, also heavier than thin Freddy. Some weekends, they played on the beach and made forts out of sand. They even looked for treasure, things beachgoers left behind. They were good buddies. Five months into the school year,

Summer Breeze entered their classroom. With a sweet and lovely smile, she was like Freddy in a way, new to the school, while Justin started in first grade in this school. Puppy love hit his heart. Got to love it. It's love, right? Justin had a crush on the same girl. She had long blond hair and green eyes and a little nose, but it's her smile that made Freddy's heart skip a beat. It's that lightning-running-through -your-veins kind of love. As the school year was coming to an end, Freddy felt the desire to get a kiss from Summer, and Justin did not want to be left out of the picture. They disputed who should ask her if she would give them a kiss. After doing rock, scissor, paper three times, it was up to Freddy to ask. He was a little frightened, but it was what he wanted in the first place. Right after he asked, her smile melted his little heart. She said yes!

After school on the way home, they all walked together: two boys and a girl having that first taste of love with a kiss. They found an open garage, and there was a car in it, so they walked to the front where it was darker. Yes! Justin and Freddy disputed on who would go first, but Summer said Freddy first. Her face was as beautiful as day. Freddy would remember his first kiss with Summer Breeze. His first kiss, he would hold it close to his heart, as he did with all his encounters with girls to come. Love was very precious. It meant a lot to him at a very youthful age. "Love is a beautiful thing, so beautiful. It makes your heart sing, so beautiful" (Young Rascals).

"Love in your heart wasn't put there to stay, love is not love till you give it away" (Oscar Hammerstein II).

As soon as school was out, the family moved again, this time outside the city, away from the beach. Dad moved the family to the top of a hill. It must have been 150 feet high. It was beautiful going up the long and winding road, which led to the house. The house was right on the side of the hill. Surrounded by nature, it was breathtaking. Here you could look out for miles and miles over the whole valley, then more hills. Their street was the first stop on the way up the hill, only three homes on the block. On the top of the hill, there were only a dozen houses around them. The presence of God was with the young lad, here on top of the world.

All summer, he went hiking all over the surrounding hills. He did not care that he had no friends. It was God and him, and they were having fun exploding. This beats any video game a kid could play today. This was real! It was hands-on fun, climbing to the top of some tall trees, getting into spots where you could not be sure how to get out, and there was no one to hear you if you yell for help. He came across rattlesnakes, foxes, all kinds of animals. He found many dinosaurs' bones, including large bipedal and quadruped forms, but back then, he had no clue about dinosaurs. He can relive it in his mind each night in bed, being the young brave cowboy, seeking out the unknown. Hallelujah! It was fun, but that Summer Breeze love was still thought of.

Down in the valley were farmers, some stores, three schools (first to sixth, seventh to ninth, and tenth to twelfth), and the city folks.

The sunrises or the sunsets have so many colors, and the shapes of the clouds were beautiful.

The days went by slowly, but the night sky had so many stars and went by quick. The beauty of it all took his mind off the deep blue sea.

"Time seemed to stand right still. In a child's world, it always will" (Moody Blues).

School started from 9:00 a.m. till 3:00 p.m. The bus did not come up the hill. Freddy and his big sister had to walk down the hill to the bus stop. They left the house at eight. That was not so bad. It was always cool in the morning, and the kids were going down the hill. What was tough? You guess it. Walking up that hill after school with lots of books, five days a week in the afternoon heat was tough for a nine-year-old boy coming from the flat beach. That's right, backpacks were not yet around for kids either. The kids started each day in school with the pledge to the flag and a song. When the school kids sang the "Battle Hum of the Republic" for the first time and came to the words, "My eyes have seen the glory of the coming of the Lord," the Holy Spirit is pouring love into his heart. Freddy's little heart was engulfed with love, and he had to fight hard to hold back bursting into tears of joy and cry out loud how he loved the Lord. They did not sing that song every day, maybe once a month, but when they did, Christ's love would fill up his heart. It would move him the same way holding back the tears of joy but feeling the love of God. When it came for Freddy to pick a song, he'd pick that one, to feel the joy of love in his heart. Christ's love is the best love of all.

School was fun at recess but hard with his dyslexia. He tried so hard, but he could not see it. Each letter by itself no problem, but put them together in a word, big problem, even the word *the* was hard to remember or spell.

There was no connection working in the mind for him. In his mind was a dead zone when looking at words. Pictures were very helpful for learning, and always moving the family to a new area and always going to new schools did not help the problem.

Days went by, and at the bus stop, Freddy met Jerry. Jerry's dad was the caretaker of the farm across the road at the bottom of the hill where they would catch the bus. On weekends, he would help Jerry with his chores around the farm. It was challenging work, and Jerry had to do it every day, before school and after it. Jerry was in the Cub Scouts and the 4H Club. He asked Freddy to join both. They had fun in the Cub Scouts, but a month later, they joined the Boy Scouts because of their age. The scouts met once a week at Jerry's house. They had an exciting time in both. You had to work for the badges to put on your shirt.

The 4H Club was more hands-on. You picked a project that you will work on for months, then at the Del Mar racetrack was the big fair held once a year. People would sell whatever you worked on. This once-a-year event, with boys and girls from around the USA, 4H Club members getting together to share stories and see their projects. Jerry had gone to the fair, when he was still in his mother's belly. Jerry's project was to raise a calf, but he did that on the farm every day, anyway. Freddy raised a baby lamb doing this was real hands on work. As soon as the baby lamb comes out of her mother's womb Freddy help raise her. Three days a week after school he would clean out the stall, brush the lamb, then put in the feed and give her a hug. The wool on her was soft and fluffy. After saying goodbye to Jerry, it's time now to walk up the hill to go home. There was dinner, then homework, then spelling words he'd work on every night, then time for his prayers, then bed.

Three months after, he took care of the lamb and watched her grow into the wooly sheep. She was big, fat, and full of wool. Then she became old enough to be sold at the state fair. School was out. Freddy's dad never got involved with anything he did. He's out making money for the big family. Mother spent most of the time with one of his three sisters. One turned out to be allergic to lots of foods and, mostly, to the pollen in the air.

When it's time for the fair to begin, he rode with Jerry, his mom, and two sisters. The girls sat in the front seat, and the boys were in the back. The car was a 1951 Ford, with no radio. They talked for a while. Then Freddy just stared out the open windows with a song going on in his mind, and the love for Summer Breeze. There wasn't a girl who thrilled his heart in this new school like she did. Freddy's mother's car had a radio, and Mom and Dad liked music as well. They played music all the time.

Jerry's dad and his big brother were in the Ford truck, pulling the trailer with the animals. The ride was about three hours to the fairgrounds. California was so open in 1958. Vehicles moved on public roads, and the traffic lights were few and far between.

They drove to the back of the fair where the animals could get out, and into their pins or stalls. The boys and the father took care of the animals, and the mother with daughters got the suitcases out of the car, and into the dorm rooms were the boys would stay for two weeks at the big fair grounds, boys taking care of their animals. At the end of two weeks, the parents and sisters would come back to the fair to watch the auction, where the animals would be sold. Hugs and prayer, then goodbyes. For the next two weeks, they would be on their own. It was Freddy's first time without his family around. Jerry did it last year with his big brother, who was there to keep an eye on the boys.

Every day in the morning, between six and eight, they had breakfast. It was in a big tent with hundreds of tables and chairs for 4H people from all around the USA. Lunch at twelve o'clock till two, and dinner at five till seven each day with all animal lovers and artists in the 4H club. After breakfast, the boys cleaned the stalls of their animals, and then feed them. The first day the smell knocked you over, some people did not keep their animals stall as clean, but it grows on you after that. Clean the poops off their butt's and feet, then brushes them down two times each day, and as the week went by seems like the wool got thicker. Fair goers would be walking around seeing all the different animals the boys and girls raised, and could be sold, plus all the rides and games. 4H members got a ID to ride the rides for free, but they had to pay a nickel or a dime for the games. You could win a prize. Back then money was worth a lot.

When chores were over, the days and the nights was theirs to do what they liked. They were different curfews for each age group. Jerry's older brother hung out with the men and could stay out late. Jerry and Freddy's age group was 9:00 p.m. in dorm room, and by 9:30 p.m., it was lights out. The wakeup call was at 5:30 each morning. The boys walked around the fair and rode the rides every day but played the games sparingly because there was little money.

A week went by, and Jerry had to help his brother pick up bales of hay for the sheep, cows, and one prize bull. Freddy was eating lunch without his best friend, but he was chatting with the other kids at the table. After he put his trash in the can and put up his tray and silverware, he turned around and looked into a pair of pretty blue eyes. Here he goes again, falling into puppy love. She had the same feelings. They exchanged names.

There were fireworks that night, and they watched those while holding hands. Boy! Love is great; kiss that Summer Breeze goodbye! He had no clue about sex. Just holding hands was magical. One of the songs that came out that year and was played on the radio a lot was "Pretty Blue Eyes." Freddy would sing it and think of her.

"Pretty blue eyes, won't you come out and play, so I can tell you what I have to say. That I love you, love you, Pretty blue eyes. Saw you from my window. My heart skip a beat. Saw you from my window. Now I have to meet, Pretty blue eyes."

For the next few days, they did everything the fair had to offer. He had the opportunity to give her a kiss, one evening, but he froze. He's only ten. What did he know? Only that his heart was saying, "I love you, love you. Oh, how I love you, Pretty Blue Eyes." You can't get enough of this energy; it was like lightning going through your veins. Each night, he went to bed singing in his mind "Pretty Blue Eyes." He couldn't wait for morning. The next day, she did not show up at breakfast. He walked over to the girls' dorms. He asked, "Have you seen April? April showers?" The young teenage girls told him her parents picked her up. Early this morning, there was a death in the family. His heart was broken, and it was painful. He did not get to say his goodbye or give her a kiss. Hindsight is always 20/20. The pain of losing someone you love causes your heart so much pain; it is one of the worst feelings.

"If a thought comes to you to do a kindness to someone do it that very minute don't put it off don't what, what's the use of doing a kindness if you do it a day to late" (Gilbert Hay).

He spent the rest of the time at the fair with Jerry and the animals. He was bummed out. His heart was hurting, and he didn't feel this way about Summer Breeze. The last day came for the selling the animal, his turn came, and the young lad was getting ready to show his sheep. He took her into the big pen, and sitting at the stands were the buyers surrounding, looking in at him and his sheep. Since it was his first time, he was very nervous as he walked her around three times in a circle for all to see. "The sheep hears his voice and follows." He's a little frightened with the crowd of people looking at him. He stopped and went down on one knee, one hand under the chin and the other at the tail end. His sheep was behaving well. He heard the auctioneer yelling out, "Do I hear ten dollars for this fine animal?" A hand with a petal went up. "Do I hear twelve? Do I hear fifteen? It ended with "Sold at thirty-nine dollars and fifty cents." That was a decent price for a sheep in those days, because you could buy a coke for a nickel back then! He walked the sheep back to her pen and hugged and kissed her on the head for the last time. He did not know what the new owner will use her for, more than likely, her wool. Jerry's dad was surprised how much the sheep sold for, and his prize bull. Jerry and Freddy made the small newspaper with their pictures.

The fair was over, and the ride home seemed longer. All he thought about was Pretty Blue Eyes, and he sang the song in his mind over and over. She liked him for his blue eyes.

He still had money in the bank. So he planned a party where guests got a turn to win a gift like at the fair, but it's free. He spent half of his money from the selling of the sheep. He had all kinds of games to play—shoot the BB gun at cans twenty feet away, throw a ball the furthest, pin the tail on the donkey was a hit, and others. The winner of each game would get a very nice gift. Fun was had by all, and Mother made a big cake and Kool-Aid. This was his best party because he gave instead of getting.

On the last day of school, Freddy and his sister got off the bus and started to walk up the hill on the long and winding road. They decided to walk up the path through the high weeds and trees, instead of the road, a shortcut coming up to the house. The path had been used many times, but this time, his sister almost stepped on a big fat snake. Freddy saw her and yelled, "Snake!" Barbara jumped over and ran, as did he. When they got to the side of the house, he told her it was a long fat snake, it might have been a rattlesnake. They were so happy they did not step on it. When they went inside, Mother, who was then pregnant, told everyone, "We must pack. The family is moving." The youngest sister had a bad reaction to all the pollen on the hill. They must move back to the beaches. The family moved to a duplex on the bay in San Diego. It was a small place for a family with four kids and a baby. Freddy and his oldest sister would walk along the bay to church every Sunday. He loved going. The Holy Spirit was working in him. The sad part was when the teachers called on him to read scripture. He could not do it without messing up. All the kids would look at him, and some would say, "He can't read." His sister read like a songbird, but his dyslexia got the better of him, but he stills went every Sunday the entire summer. He wanted so much to be able to read the Bible, God's Word.

School was about to start. So what happens they move again close to the beach? They lived on the first floor in an apartment complex, a block from the beach in the city of Chula Vista. Freddy was in the sixth grade a month away from eleven. He's very shy in school because of his reading problem. He barely passed the fifth grade. It's 1960, and the teenagers were kissing and going to parties, dancing to "The Twist" by Chubby Checker and having all kinds of fun.

The transistor radio came out, and lots of people had them, and they were all rockin' and rollin'. He was watching and waiting for a friend to play with. He knew he was loved by his family and his heavenly Father but needed a buddy to hang with. Then he met Benjamin. He was taller and thin, with blond hair and blue eyes, and he had braces. His father was in the air force and was not around much. Freddy's dad was only around on weekends. Because of work, he was always on the road. Who knew what he did? His dad could talk a person into or out of anything. When you saw him, you wanted to be his friend. He had lots of charm. This is the year another girl was born into the family, and Freddy's dad had business in Japan for over two months after her birth.

One of Ben's hobbies was saving records—78s and 45s from the '40s, '50s, and now '60s. He had hundreds of them in his spare room. His mother was pretty and nice. Freddy never met Ben's dad, but Ben had a picture of him in his bedroom. He looked like his dad.

Ben and Freddy did a lot of things together. They became best friends. Sometime in November, the young lad was invited to go to the mountains with Ben and his mother. The car was an aqua green 1957 Chevy, with a radio. They thought they were the cat's meow they both had leather jacket, black with zippers all over. The ride up the mountain was an enjoyable time had by all. Seeing lots of nature and every so often an eye-opener; a shoot of how high you really are looking out to valley below, seeing clouds at your level and hilltops, the whole picture of God's creation looking out the window. "Look out of my window see the world spinning by, see the look in her eye" (Moody Blues).

We're going around the open bend. When they drove into a parking area, the boys played in the snow as Ben's mother looked on, alone in a daze, but looked at them. But then there was a shout. "Mom! Mom! Come on! Throw a snowball!" After she throws one, it is a free for all. Then Freddy stopped and just looked at the beauty of it all. Mother Nature and Mother Nature's son—he felt one with God, and he knew he was. The sun was setting. It was hard to take it all in—the light, the balance, magnificent perfection. Then there was the evening; there were so many stars it would take your cooled breath away. He'd ask, "Father, can I see a shooting star?" Zoom! One passed by. "Thank you!" The boys even got to go to the observatory and see the telescope that looked deep into the heavens.

"Love all God's creation both the whole and every grain of sand, love every leave every ray of light. Love all the animals, love all the plants, love each separate thing. If you love each thing you will perceive the mystery of God in all" (Dostoevsky).

Going down the mountain was the same as going up; they had an enjoyable time together. There was music on the radio, laughter, and friendship. They were just making memories.

Freddy met his other friend Saul in school; he lived in the same apartment complex but not as close as Ben. Saul was smart and as tall as Freddy with a gap in his front teeth. He had brown eyes, and his hair was short with little bangs on his forehead. Saul had no hobbies like Benjamin, but Saul's dad came home every day from work. He was a family man. One Sunday, Saul's dad took the boys to see one of the San Diego Chargers football games. You can look at it as what a young man of the Roman times would have felt being in a coliseum in Rome to see his first battle of the gladiators.

Freddy fell in love with football. He started to play it all the time. He was hooked; he wanted to be a football player. He got shower pads and a helmet. He played with other kids who had shower pads and helmets at an accessible area at the apartment complex. It was not far from the swimming pool area. His dad was never around to do anything with him, and his close relationship with his heavenly Father now only involved a prayer at night, and not on his knees anymore. He was thinking about football, girls, and music. His mind was going earthly all the way. In the apartment complex where he lived were lots of teenagers. Back then, one year made a substantial difference. Freddy just turned eleven. He's not allowed to hang out with the older kids. They had dance parties on Friday nights. He walked in on one party. "Let's Twist Again Like We Did Last Summer" was playing, which just came out on the radio. Everyone was having fun, and no one cared he was there dancing.

Just four months since school started, the family moved again—not just in another part of town but out of the state of California! It's the Christmas break. They would be on the road again.

# Chapter 3

## To Our Children's Children's Children!

"Through the eyes of a child, you will come out to see, that your world is spinning around, and through life you will be, a small part of a hope of a love that excites, through the eyes of a child you will see."

(Moody Blues)

Dad goes on ahead with a friend in his car to Texas. Mother with the four kids and a baby must pack up all their things that would fit into a very big U-Haul trailer, which would be attach to the bumper of the car. They are on the road, driving east. Big sister must take her two mice in a cage. The young lad and his older sister are so tired of moving. All they know is they will meet Dad somewhere in Texas. Freddy has the front seat with the newborn baby sister. He's thinking, "When will Mom have a boy? Enough of the girls." With three sisters in the backseat and the two mice in a cage on the floorboard, it was tight. The first day goes by without problems. Mother is a good driver. The traffic in California has taught her well. They drive in the dark and then stop at a motel. All of them are tired from the long drive and fall into a deep sleep, even the baby, thank God. Sometime in the night, Mommy mouse gives birth to six babies. In the morning, big sis is so excited, as are the other children; they have all seen animals giving birth, goes back to Texas with all the animals they had.

With the busyness of the morning, Mother carries the one-month old in her arms and tells all the kids, "Get ready!" They just finish eating cereal in the hotel room. Everyone helps to pick up things, and by nine, they are out of the parking lot on the road.

About four hours into the ride, the right rear tire blows, and the car and trailer do a 360-degree turn on the highway. They end up on the side of the road, facing the right direction, east. Time seems to stand quite still for all in the car. That 360-degree spin is less than five seconds. It is like the teacup ride in Disney World, five kids turning that wheel. You can go around fast. A very kind man stops his car behind us and comes over and sticks his head into the car. "Is everyone all right!" He tells Mother he has never seen anything like that before. The car and the U-Haul trailer spins completely around in a circle!

The car stops on the shoulder, facing the flow of traffic. That does not happen every day of the week! "God is with you all. That's a miracle, I'd tell you!" No one is hurt, not even the mice. Another man comes over, and they both change the tire as they all stand off the road, and they all thank God and the men who helped them.

Sometime in the late-night hours, they meet Dad in a hotel in Texas. In the morning, Dad's friend drives back to California, and the family heads east, driving all day and into the night. The young lad would stay up, watching the darkness go by. Then in the distance, he'd see a beam of light coming at them, then a car's headlights flying by. Then late in the night, they get a room. The next day, hours into the drive, Mother tells the children, "We're heading back to Philadelphia." Finally, a rest stop. Dad pulls off the road, and they all use the restrooms, and Mother puts together something to eat at a picnic table. Then they are on the road again, driving all day long. Dad loves driving with one hand on the wheel. He smokes with the other. He does it so well. He's a cool-looking man. Because they are going east, night comes on them quick. Again, the lad is sitting up, looking out the window, and seeing in the distance the big bright beams of lights shooting up the hill. At first, he's not sure what it is; he has never been on a highway in the mountains like this at night. Could it be a spaceship? Outside, it is so dark. He sees that it's a big semitruck with lights all over the front, the sides, and back. Now he knows there is nothing to be afraid of. Hours go by; Dad pulls up in front of a church. No one knows why. He tells Mother, "I am going to see the pastor."

When Dad walks back to the car, he seems upset. He tells Mother the pastor would not help them. If the minister walks out to the car and sees the five kids, then maybe he would have some compassion and help. After Dad gets into the car, he does not say anything much, but you'd know he is thinking it: "Where is God when you need him?" The kids are left in the dark. Parents do not tell the children all the problems they are having in life. Mom and Dad do not fight in front of the kids, more likely because Dad is not around much out and is working all the time.

The Holy Spirit moves Freddy's heart and puts in his mind the reason Dad stopped: they needed gas money to keep going. Dad and Mom have no money. In those days, credit cards did not exist back then; there were only checks if you had a bank account.

Freddy tells his dad he has money and where it is. It just so happens that Freddy had two two-dollar bills, three silver dollars, two silver half dollars, and some dimes and nickels in his box of special collectibles, inside the U-Haul trailer by the back doors. He had gotten the idea to start collecting old money because of his friend Benjamin and his old record collection. Gas is between fifteen and twenty-five cents a gallon. Father drives on, then stops at the first gas station, and talks to the owner who lived in the house behind the station. Dad talks the man into giving him money for the collectibles, plus a full tank of gas and snacks; they have enough gas to drive all night long. That morning, they stop at a diner so Mother can clean up the kids and buy some breakfast—the cheapest meal you could buy. The big kids know how to go without food; it has happened a few times in the past. As Tuesday afternoon comes, the family is in Philly, not far from Mother's sister's home. You can feel the difference in the road. It's bumpier. It's made of cobblestones. Soon, they pull up to the same house he visited nine years ago, to see his grandmother and grandfather. It's a three-story house, where Freddy's mother grew up. Uncle Stan and Aunt Cass own it now. They welcome the family with smiles. Aunt Cass is a heavyset woman but with a beautiful face, long black hair that reaches her butt, and a happy laugh. Uncle Stan is tall and strong looking, and he works in a plant where they build helicopters. He works the night shift. The homes are all side by side, up and down the stone street. The homes are all the same, cement stairs going up to the porch, walking up about seventeen steps onto a porch five foot wide about twenty-five feet long, with an old swinging chair not far from the right side of the front door; so to swing on it, you would be looking at the chairs and table on your porch, and behind you are your neighbors and their porches.

When Freddy walks into the house, flashbacks fill his mind. He sees himself at four, sitting on grandfather's knee, taking a sip of his beer. He can even smell it in his mind. The parents are chatting in the kitchen. Freddy sits down on the sofa and ponders about the past. This is the city where he heard the voice, and his mind was opened, then living five years in the wide-open spaces of Texas, then three years with the beauty of the beaches, the sunsets living on the ocean or the hills with the sunrises, all the beautiful times on the farm and 4H, and now he's here, in the city with no life, darkness all around, no trees, no ocean, only old buildings and pigeons, dirty streets, and the air smells. The good times they go by so quick. Freddy would remember the time the family drove up the coast of California and how beautiful that trip was, and then the two times they all drove to Tawana, Mexico, and watched a bullfight and spent three days in a very charming hotel on the beach.

One week of staying in the house feels like a month. His aunt gives him ten cents. There is a store around the block; the young lad is going for the first time without someone in the family going, as well. In Texas or California, he could ride his bike all over the place, with no problems. Here! It could be a problem.

Leaving the house and walking down the seventeen steps onto the sidewalk, he then walks north for three blocks and turns left, and he walks into the corner store. The smell of fresh bread fills the air. He walks around and looks at the fruits, meat, the dead fish, pickles in a big wooden barrel, and even the people. After getting a Tootsie Roll lollipop, some Dots, and a Snickers, all that for a dime. He leaves the corner store, putting the goodies in his pockets, but he puts one Tootsie in his mouth and throws away the little brown paper bag and lollipop rapper in the trash. He's a happy little guy for now. As he turns at the corner on his street, he sees a group of young guys not far away, walking toward him. The biggest boy stops Freddy, saying, "I want to fight you, or give me your money!" He looks like the toughest of them all.

"For it is not you that speaks, but the Spirit of your Father which speeketh in you" (Matthew 10:20).

The Holy Spirit comes into Freddy's mind and fills him with the right words to say. All the boys just stare at him as he speaks. After less than two minutes, he walks away without engaging in a fight, and some friends and all his candies are still in his pockets, and he sucks on his Tootsie. Hallelujah! God is good; God is great. Let us thank him for this candy, amen.

He is not thinking of the Lord before he got the candy, but after being saved, he thanks the Lord.

This is the city of brotherly love? This is hell for the boy. This sojourn has brought him back thinking of his heavenly Father. He prays day and night: "Father, please get us out of this old city, and back on the beach, please! Thank you. Thank you. Thank you. Amen. A thank you for the Holy Spirit, Son, and Father." He starts to understand they are one. He knows God loves him because of the voice and his past blessings.

The young lad sleeps in the same bed as his aunt, but he is asleep by the time she gets into bed. His aunt is a very good artist; she has drawings of animals or people around the house. In the mornings, the lad would go down stairs to the kitchen to eat a healthy breakfast and do the regular bathroom chores, then down to the basement. It is grandpa's old plumbing shop. Grandpop's lab has all the tools and supplies. He spends hours there playing. The house has a backyard, but it is small. It snowed one weekend, just enough to make some snowballs, and he thinks back when he threw snow at his friend Ben and how much room there was in the past and the beauty of it all.

After three weeks, the family is on the road again. Mother's youngest brother comes along. The car is packed with souls, but there is no U-Haul trailer! Dad sold everything to have money to get out of town. He tells the kids, "We are moving to Florida," and two days later, they are in Orlando, Florida. Dad leaves everyone at a park to eat. He goes to rent a fully furnished house. Freddy is so happy God is answering his prayer, and life is moving right along. He's on the road to get there. "Next to knowing is knowing where to find out" (Dr. J Vern McGee).

The kids are enrolled to finish the last four months of school; they already miss too much. Freddy is so far behind, and they are studying subjects he has never heard of. The only subject he can relate to is math. With his dyslexia, he is just getting his addition, subtraction, and division down. Now they're throwing fractions at him. Now and then he sees the numbers in the right way, but words, not as much. He is lost in school. In his mind the letters together are not connecting. He would sit in the back so he would not be picked for anything, but he is always making friends.

Orlando was all woods and lakes, and the houses were more open. They were not right next to each other like in Philly. It was very hot, like no other place he ever lived no ocean. There were no foothills.

One of Freddy's friend in school was Mat. They would go to a small lake and fish on an old rotten dock some Saturdays. The boys kept the worms they dug up in a can and put the can on the ground just before the dock. They didn't want the worms to fall into the water, because the dock was old and parts were missing. They had been sitting on the dock, fishing for thirty minutes. Freddy needed another worm. He lost his worm with the many bites, but he was hooking none. He walked very carefully to the front of the dock and grabbed a couple of worms. He turned around to walk back to the dock. He saw a snake—a cottonmouth crawling up the wooden post just behind Matthew. He yelled,

"Mat, a snake!" Mat turned to see. Right then with his cane pole, Freddy wiped it at the snake, and the hook hit the snake, right on top of the head. The angels had to be guiding that hook, because the snake fell into the lake and took off fast. Mat jumped up and hopped as fast as he can off to an old broken dock, to his buddy. He thanked him, and the boys went back to the house with no fish, but they were happy no one got hurt. They never fished after that. The big reason was by the beginning of summer the family moved out of this hot city. Dad's new place! Daytona Beach. Yes! Thank you, God, they were back on the beach. Hallelujah! Well! Not on the beach, but five blocks away from the beach.

The months before school starts, the young lad visits the beach by riding his bike. His first day, to his surprise! You can ride bikes and cars drive on the beach here as well. Here is another surprise: there is a boardwalk with rides, games, shops, and food. Riding up and down the beach, he collects soda glass bottles, one bottle is sold for five cents. Five cents adds up to a dollar quick, and a dollar buys a lot in the sixties. Every day, he rides up and down the beach.

He also receives an allowance of fifty cents for all the chores he does around the house—mowing the lawn, taking out the trash, shining five pairs of his dad's shoes, keeping his room clean, and sweeping the carport. Talk about underpaid, but there are times Dad gives him an extra dollar. Great—off to bowling and soda and hamburger.

Summer is almost over, and his mother is going to enroll the kids into school. Freddy thinks he's going into seventh grade, but there is a problem: the move from California to Philly and then to Orlando. He misses too much school, and he must do sixth grade over again. It is his reading, his dyslexia. None of his sisters are kept back. This does not bother him, because he knows no one will know he is doing sixth over again. He's one of the new kids in school again.

As school gets going, he rides his bike every day, rain or shine. After chores on Saturdays, the fun begins with friends—bowling at the plaza, games at the boardwalk, and fishing on the canal; and every Sunday, Mom cooks good breakfast, Dad reads the paper, and the kids do their own thing. As ten o'clock came around, the family get ready for church. This is the year John Glenn goes into orbit around the earth, and Cape Canaveral is the place to be. John Kennedy is the president, and it would be another eleven years before Disney World would be in Orlando. They have been going to a Baptist church for about six Sundays. This Sunday is special for Freddy. The preacher is giving a calling for all to come to accept Christ and to be baptized.

"And because you are sons, God has sent forth the Spirit of his Son into your hearts, crying Abba, Father" (Galatians 4:6).

He's heart is moved big-time. He's being called, and he feels the Spirit moving him to walk up. He looks up at his dad! He gives him the nod. "I agree with your decision, son!" That nod his father gives helps that fever that could have held him back. It's gone, and he walks up to give his life to Jesus the Christ of God.

"The best thing a Father can do for his children is helping them to know Jesus the Christ of God." His dad might not have done a lot with his son, but this one thing is the best a dad could do. "Listen, we think we have found you. Listen, we think we have seen you" (Moody Blues).

The young lad is the only one who walks up to give his life to Christ that Sunday. A prayer then ended the service. The pastor told the young Freddy and his mother, "Next week, you will be baptized. You will be laid into water at the end of the service. Make sure you bring your swimsuit." The boy really does not know what this baptism in water is all about, and he does not ask either. These are the first steps to a never-ending love, and it's right around the corner.

That week, he tells some school friends who live within a block that he is going to be baptize at church. They make fun of it, but that does not bother Freddy. His reading problem keeps him from reading his Bible to learn more about God and his Christ. "There is one body, and one Spirit, even as you are called in one hope of your calling; one Lord one faith, one baptism, one God, and Father of all, who is above all, and through all, and in you all. But unto every one of us is given grace according to the measure of the gift of Christ" (Ephesians 4:4–7).

On the morning of the seventh Sunday, the family put on their Sunday's best. Mother gets to wear a pretty dress, as all the girls do. Freddy is the only one excited about going. They arrive at church a little early so the pastor could show the boy where to go and what to do at the end of the service, when he will put him under the water. The family sits down—Dad, the eldest daughter, the third, fourth, and Mother with youngest daughter on her lap, then Freddy. They sit near the back so when it's time to go out the door, the boy will not disturb the service. He gets the sign from the pastor, and he goes through the back side door. He walks down a long hallway with doors on left side; at the end is his room, on the right. He takes off his shirt, and in his pants he had put his underwear in the pocket at home to put on after the baptism he wore his bathing suit under his dress pants. He slips into the white robe, then stands at the closed door where the pastor asks him to wait. It's darker where he's standing. The young boy can hear the pastor talking while he is behind the door. Freddy is asking Christ to come into his heart but has no glue what is going to happen to him after this life-changing experience. Then the door is open, and the light is let in, and he walks into the *light*. He's looking at all the people looking at him. He's a little frightened seeing all these eyes on him. The pastor comes around and puts his arm on his shoulder. He is comforted. They walk up the steps, then down into the big tub. The water is so cold. they walk slowly to the center almost to the boy's shoulders. Then the pastor said, "Son, you have asked Jesus Christ to come into your life." The church people are just looking on. It's so quiet. Then the pastor said, "In the name of the Father, Son, and Holy Spirit." As he said Spirit, the pastor laid him back into the water. The boy is holding his nose with the same fingers he would use picking up a crawdad. Then going under the water and being lifted up again standing up. He looks out at the people, and they're all smiling and praising God. Some say, "Hallelujah!" The pastor and the boy walk up the steps out of the tub of water. The pastor smiles and tells the young boy, "Jesus is with you," and he leaves to go to the front door to thank the people. As they leave the church, he is still half wet.

The boy dries off and changes into his clothes, not feeling any different, and walks out to the car. As the family drives home from church, not one asks him any questions. Dad pulls up the driveway, stops, puts the car in park, and turns off the car. The family gets out of the car. Freddy gets out of the car last. As soon as he steps on the ground, he feels this bubble of love surrounding him, and he starts feeling a strong love in his heart. This love inside gets stronger as he takes a couple more steps. It's better than any love he has ever known. All the puppy love in the past—Summer Breeze, April Showers— cannot compare to what he feels inside now, and all around him is a feeling of protective love. It's all too beautiful. When he walks, he feels this bubble around him like an energy force of love.

This love engulfs him. It's so strong. He is so full of love. He thinks he should tell someone. He cannot touch this bubble of love or energy, but he feels the strong presence of the Holy Spirit all around him, but he does not know it's the Holy Spirit. He only feels the presence of love within and outside his body.

"But the Lord watches over those who fear him, those who rely on his unfailing love. He rescues them from death and keeps them alive in times of famine. We put our hope in the Lord. He is our shield. In him our hearts rejoice, for we trust in his Holy name. Let your unfailing love surround us, Lord for our hope is in you alone" (Psalm 33:18–22). God has covered the young boy with love.

"This is how we know that he lives in us: We know it by the Spirit he gave us" (John 3:24). He does not go in the house. Instead, he rides his bike over to his friend's. The bubble of love energy is all around him as he is riding, even as he is walking up to the front door. All around him, he feels loved and has a peace of mind. It is so wonderful. The mother tells him that the boys are in the backyard playing. He walks thru the house with the energy force of love, excited to tell his friends about his love for Jesus. Then one of the boys said, "Jesus is stupid! You're stupid to believe." The other brother starts a fight with his brother for saying what he said. Freddy is watching them, still surrounded with the bubble of love. This energy force of joy is unspeakable. He goes over to stop the fight, and as soon as he touches the one brother on the shoulder to stop the fighting, the Spirit of love leaves him. He feels this energy—this Spirit, this bubble of love that is all around him and in him, from the bottom of his feet through his body, then out of the top of his head. It feels like a mighty rush from the force of love. Zoom, it's gone, and he stops and just looks upward. The boys stop pushing each other and look up also, and they both say, "What are you looking at, Freddy?"

He does not say a word, walks out the back wooden gate, and goes to the front gets on his bike, and goes home. For the rest of the day, he talks to no one, only thinking of that love that surrounds him, the feeling in his heart, being all loved; it is so wonderful how he has this covering of love, energy, but now it is gone, because he touched the boys of anger. One thing he does not know as of now, the Holy Spirit will never leave you or forsake you, and from this point on, he will be raised on Christ's love, not by Dad or Mom but by the Holy Spirit. Freddy knows for sure God is real, and he is loved by him. Then he thinks about the voice when he was a baby and how his mind was opened. He is blessed now. He is a boy after God's heart.

A couple of weeks have gone by. It's a Saturday, and one of the older boys who lived in the neighborhood who does not hang with Freddy, but Freddy has seen him time and again in the neighborhood. He knows the brothers, and now he stops over, and Freddy is there. He tells them he has an idea on how to get some squirt guns. He tells the boys he has a plan. "We are going to go to the five-and-ten-cent store in the plaza. We will go into the store minutes apart. When you first go in, you buy a five-cent bag of popcorn and eat half of it. You walk around the store, taking your time and looking at different things. Then when you walk by the toys, put a squirt gun into your half-eaten popcorn bag. When you boys see me go out of the store, the next boy goes over and then slowly walks out of the store."

As he tells them what to do, Freddy hears a small voice just like the one when he was a baby. "No, don't steal." He tells the boys he's not going. They all call him chicken and tell him he will not be their friend anymore. He's does not want to lose his friends. He's not a chicken. So he said okay. Everything goes as the older boy has told them to do. Freddy is last to come out of the store, and the boys all ride their bikes over to the brother's house to fill the guns and squirt water at each other. As Freddy is filling up his gun, the water is coming out. There is a big hole under the trigger. It's a defect, and water just runs out as you fill it. The Holy Spirit tells him, "You should not steal." He feels so bad inside. He tells God he is sorry. He makes a vow that he will not steal again. The tempter will come, and he would like us to fail. He has to pay attention and open those ears to the Holy Spirit. He wants us to succeed. Thank you, Lord.

He stops hanging with these boys and starts going after school to a recreation hall for kids. He learns how to play chess. He's good for his age, and he starts to play football again with boys at the recreation center. One of his new friends is Johnathan. He likes fishing.

On weekends, they would camp out at Johnathan's grandparents' house. It's on the canal on the beach side, a three-story home painted white with green trim, a porch all around the house, a big yard; and in the back is where they camp. At midnight, they would go to the kitchen and get a Dr. Pepper in a bottle out of the refrigerator, then get into their little boat in the river, staying close to shore. No motor. They would paddle everywhere just fishing, talking, and enjoying the silence of the night the stars big and bright. This is a very good year of fun with new friends. The young Freddy is very happy knowing God's love.

School is coming to the end, and the family is moving ten miles north to Ormond Beach right on the beach side. The love of the Lord was very real, and he thought of God' love. The best time was when he watches the sun rising on the beach and saying a prayer and taking in the beauty of it all. He has never told anyone of the bubble of love; he does not want to hear anyone be negative about his real love for God.

Let's give you a fast rundown on Freddy's life. Born in Philly and lived their three years in the same house. Moved to Texas and lived there for five years in the same house and went to the same school. Moved to California and moved four times in three years and three different schools. His dyslexia problem unknown then to him, but only his mother knew he had a reading problem. Then in the month of November 1960, they moved to Philly and stayed their three weeks. They moved to Florida, to the city of Orlando, and lived there for four months going to a new school, then to Daytona Beach for nine months. He attended a new school, then moved to Ormond Beach, two months. In August of 1964, Dad moved his family down the cost of Florida to Fort Lauderdale.

The population is about five hundred thousand or more in Broward County, but it's spread all around the vast area. They move into a house across the street from the beach. The house is cool. It's big for a family of five kids, with a baby on the way. Freddy gets his own room. His big sister gets hers as well. There are just ceiling fans in the house with the windows open and the ocean breeze. Not too many homes have air conditioners, but it is still comfortable. Across the street is a vacant lot. From the living room window, you can see the sunrise. At night, he loves hearing the crashing of the waves, which would put him to sleep. The ocean and the canals water are aqua blue; you can see the bottom and all the sea creatures in the water, boy! Fort Lauderdale was beautiful then.

Mother is pregnant with number six; Freddy is soon to be thirteen. He starts school. On the first day, he finds out there are seven different classes and gets two locks and must remember the combinations—one for his books, the other he needs for the whole hour he's in gym class.

This is all new to him. Gym—he loves this class, as most boys. He loves sports. The dream of being a football player is coming back in play. One of his classes is music. He learns to read it, write it, and play the trumpet. It was funny his dyslexia does not affect his music reading. He enjoys music. He grew up listening to Elvis and all the other men, woman, and jazz bands. His dad loves all kinds of music. He's having an exciting time in gym, art class, but reading is very difficult. Again, he makes friends. In fact, he makes a lot of friends in sports, music, and art.

In November, John F. Kennedy was shot. Freddy was in history class when the news came over the loud speaker. His teacher fought in the second world war—a strong-looking man, and the whole class saw him cry. It was a very sad day for our country.

In December, Mother gives birth to a boy. Freddy's happy, but it's a baby. Sometime in January, the family is moving again. Rent on the beach house has gone up three times of what it was in August. The snowbirds have been coming down and back in town. The good thing on this move is the kids get to stay in the same schools. This is the year the Beatles come to Miami, their music was out on the AM radio. The friends he meets in this area of town will be friends in a band of which he will be involved with this new school year. The band is good. There is an article on them in the Fort Lauderdale newspaper, and the band's name was Grim Rippers.

The school year is finished. They move again. The new house is cool, but none of his friends live around this new area of town. In fact, in this area of Fort Lauderdale, the kids go to a different junior high school. It's only a year old. Mother makes sure the kids stay in the same school.

Dad opens a restaurant on Federal Highway and calls it the Fabulous Hoagie. Freddy works in the kitchen, cutting up onions, tomatoes, and meat. He cleans all the pots and pans and dishes and sweeps and mops the floors. When his dad first opens the restaurant, he let him sit on a rocking chair on top of a round stand, and he is rocking with a hoagie in one hand and the other hand pointing to the eatery. Traffic was very light. Dad gets another great idea. They start selling tacos, and they have a drive-up window, and there is a boat dock in the back. Three months go by, and they are doing well. They hear a hurricane is on its way. Hurricane! What is that? Now the weather people could not pinpoint where it might hit in the early '60s. This one hits Fort Lauderdale, and when it's over, the restaurant is all broken up really bad.

With no insurance, Dad loses everything. This is another blow to Freddy's dad. His ideas were great, but something always goes wrong and sets him back to start, but he always has a smile for the kids. It's Mother who takes on more of the burden.

Freddy's mother is too busy with three younger kids at her feet to take him anywhere. So he sits around the house most of the time. Summer is almost over, and a new family moves in down the street. He meets the two brothers, and they hit it off well. They would hitchhike to the beach every day and body surf and check out the girls. After the beach, they would go swimming in the brother's pool. School is a week away, and Freddy uses the money he made at the restaurant to buy new clothes. His new friends would go to the new junior high school, and Freddy would go back to the one he has been going to—Sunrise Junior High. He is still doing all the same things, but in music, he wants to play the piano. No money for that, so he stops playing the trumpet, gets out of the school band. He asks the football coach if he could go out for the team, and he said, "Next year, son, and we start training in August." It's the month before school starts.

That school year, Freddy meets some friends who through the summer will learn how to play rock and roll, learning all the hit songs. He's learns music in school and hangs out with the boys. There are parties on Friday nights, all the kids from school would go. There were all the girls he meets, but very few were drinking or smoking pot.

Summer is here, and Freddy hangs out with his new buddies. They start going to the dances for fourteen-year-olds and older. The dance clubs are popping up everywhere in Broward County. There are live bands playing on Friday and Saturday nights. It costs a dollar to get in, and the place stays open till 1:00 p.m. Nonstop fun till you leave.

Every day, they go to the beach. To get there, they would walk up to a car at a traffic light. If the window is down, they ask for a ride. If the window is up, they knock on the window. In the '60s, that would work. When they arrive at the beach, it is across the street on A1A from Hugh Taylor Birch State Park. This is their spot for the next four years. The waves are never good for surfing. You have to go up the beach twenty miles for good surfing waves, but the body surfing is fun where they hung out. There is a tunnel that goes under the road to the State Park that had a restaurant.

Three months go by fast. In August, they move again. This time to New Jersey just south of Atlantic City. The old house is on the beach, and Freddy has his own room.

He works out with weights and keeps to himself. He hates this move. He's back to knowing no one. When school starts, it is so different. The kids are too. So for two months, he works hard on reading and writing, even with his dyslexia. He does better, but he longs for his friends back in Fort Lauderdale. The kids were different in New Jersey than in Florida. You are Italian, black, or a Jew. They all hang out in their own groups. Freddy has his Florida driver's license, so for fun, he drives around town, but he is out of place. He knows deep down inside this is not right. He starts to pray to the Father and asks for the family to move back to Fort Lauderdale. Freddy is very happy. God answers his prayers. During December holiday break, the family moves back to Florida. They lived in Hollywood, Florida beach in and hotel for one week, then back to Fort Lauderdale on the beach in a hotel for months they finish out the school year.

Freddy is now closer to his school. Now he can go out for the football team. Before you know it, it's August. It is hot. Football practice is hard—all the running, hitting, running, and falling on your stomach. But you get up and run, then do it all over again, and again, in the heat, which was in the nineties. Freddy is the fastest boy on the team. He's great at this sport. He can't wait till the first game. School starts, and Freddy makes lots of friends—the jocks on the football team, the greasers, surfers, and the geeks. The girls start to pay attention to him. All seem good. After the third game, Freddy talks to the head coach one on one. He asks him why he does not let him play. On the next game, he puts Freddy in as a wide end only in one game one play, then puts him on the bench. Freddy sees the head coach again. The coach tells him, "If you don't like it, kid, get your ass off the team.: The coach's son is on the team, and he doesn't want Freddy to take top billing, so the coach will not let him play in the games. He leaves the team knowing no matter how hard he tries, there is not much he can do to play in a game. The letter to put on the sweater means nothing if you do not earn it on the field of battle.

His dad is not around much to talk to. In fact, he does not know his son is on the football team. Freddy's shop teacher owns the place on the beach side. He helps him by getting him to join the track team some time in February. Months go by, and he does. Turns out, he is the fastest on the team. He's going to all the meets and wins. He's popular in school, and the girls are giving him the attention the jocks get. One of the night races, Freddy wins the race. Then his right leg popped a liniment on the inside step. Oh! The pain is dreadful. He goes down and walks out of the race. The coach yells for him to get going, but he can't move. It is painful to just walk. He loses his speed. That night, his dreams of being a football player are gone.

He gets a letter for track, and the school year ends. They move again into a large three-bedroom house in an area where they all get to go to their old schools. This is where it was as far west as you can go in the city. After that, there is only farmland and cows. Slowly, people are moving in, and it gets busy with homes starting to be built all the way to US 441Hy.

The Holy Spirit has been knocking on his heart and mind, letting him know he's here.

One day, he asks our heavenly Father, "What should I be in this life?" The Holy Spirit tells him to be a preacher. The same voice is calling. It's like in the Bible when the young man who had a lot of earthly things said, "What must I do to get eternal life?" Jesus tells him to give up everything and follow him! Just like this man, Freddy rejects this fellow Jesus and asks the Father in prayer. "I have my friends now, the ones I love. I would like my freedom to drink and have sex with girls. I can't give this up now. I will not go down this preaching road for now." The Father tells him that he would and to keep in touch with him through the Holy Spirit, who never leaves him.

It's the new year! The tenth grade at Fort Lauderdale High School. There are so many good bands and singers. Elvis, Rickie Nelson, Ray Charles, Frank Sinatra, Tony Bennet, The Beatles, The Doors, The Rolling Stones, Cream, The Spirit (who had one hit song called "Fresh Garbage"), and so many more singers and bands. The Moody Blues are a group he is yet to get to know, but their music is played on the radio. He passes the tenth grade.

It's the summer of 1967. Freddy and his friends are starting to drink more. He does not like the taste of beer but drinks it to look cool in front of the guys and the girls. They are a group of young men now. There is about eighteen of them, and out of them, only two smoke cigarettes. They hang together every weekend. Some work; some do not. They are Germans, Italians, Jews, Polish, a mix of Americans in the promised land. They feel and acts as if they are all brothers; a family-like bond is there. They are the picture of cool. They think they are smooth as silk. Three of the guys are in a band, so the band plays at the parties. The summer of love and fun goes by fast. The eleventh grade is full of dates, dances, parties, and rock and roll. No one is doing any drugs. They are only drinking. Schoolwork is hard with dyslexia but got done to make Cs and Ds.

The weekend parties are all on their minds. The question is, whose parents are going out this weekend, and for how long? They do not just party in the summer but all year long every weekend. In the summer of 1968, all the boys had jobs. They are making enough to rent a hotel room and buy beer and booze.

The key is getting enough girls to the party. This year, Freddy gets a movie camera with no sound and starts filming all that the guys do, on the weekend at the beach, parties at night, outings to races, or parks in the day. Summer is over, and it's the last year of school. The Vietnam War is on all the seniors' minds at the end of this year; you could be going. After a month of school, Freddy asks if he could go to another school, the one that most of his friends go to. It all works out, and he does go to a new high school. He falls in love with his English teacher. She is only eight years older than him. He enjoys going to her class. She is in his dreams only.

The couple of months go by without a problem. The weekends are always fun. The guys would get the rooms and booze, and set up on Friday late afternoon, then start slow with the party, close friends only talking about last week's party. Then Saturday night is the big bang! Everyone comes with dates. Everyone has an enjoyable time—singing, dancing, and laughter making movies.

The new year, 1969, comes in. A lot has happened. Freddy gets his own sports car, and weekends are more fun, but he must work to make payments. Months go by, and Freddy is introduce to a pretty girl with blonde hair, Brinda. They hit it off. They do everything together, and their love is blossoming. Most of the guys have girlfriends now, and the parties are wilder. More booze and some of the guys start smoking pot. At the end of the night, they go their separate ways, sex for all who have girl-friends. Freddy's investment in a sports car is not a clever decision. Now with payments, he works after school till midnight, and his school-work is always behind. At the end of school, he must make up a half of credit. Summer school for a mouth, and he gets his diploma. The next month, he and Brinda find out she is with child. They must tell their parents. Freddy tells his mother in the bedroom, and she cries. Dad is never around. Brinda's side of the family makes ready for an August wedding. Freddy thinks this will be the right thing to do. The new baby needs a dad. His dad is never around. He only has his heavenly Father within to lead him, but God's love is the best love ever. The wedding is attended by all his buddies and their girlfriends. His mother, brother, sisters on one side, but his dad does not come. All Brinda's family on the other side, and Freddy and Brinda, who is three months pregnant, in the middle. Everything goes well, and at the reception, it is as if it were a weekend party.

The young married couple get an apartment in Pompano. They are the first couple in the group to become man and wife, and he would still go to the parties with his pregnant wife. It's February, and the Moody Blues are playing in Miami.

Freddy has tickets. All the guys who are going are at Freddy's place, but the wife goes into labor, and off to the hospital they go with all his friends. All the guys are in the lobby, and one asks Freddy, "Are you going?" "No, I cannot go. I must see the baby."

They leave for the concert. Freddy is by himself for about two hours, looking back on his life. Another two hours later, they have a girl. Months later, the army's draft notice now reads "Deferred." Then it starts, and he goes to the parties, and she stays home. There is one time when Brinda stays home because there is no one to watch the baby. That Saturday night, he goes to the house in Margate where the weekend party is happening. All the guys who are stoned are there that night. They used to drink, but now they just smoke pot and drop LSD. They bring an album called *On a Threshold of a Dream*, by the Moody Blues. This one song, In the beginning, it moves Freddy, and the next day, he buys the first album *Days of Future Past*. This album had "Nights in White Satin," and Tuesday afternoon, these songs play a lot on the radio. With the next paycheck, he buys the second album *In Search of the Lost Cord*, and with the next paycheck, he buys the one he heard at the party *On a Threshold of a Dream*. Now he has fallen in love with the Moody Blues. Their music and words to each song are calling to him. Each album is telling a story. The whole album is woven together as one, each one different, but the meaning to each one is love in God, man, and life. He can't get enough. He plays them over and over all the time. The year goes buy quickly. He does not read his Bible, because of his dyslexia. He tries to read it, but it's hard for him. He loves knowing the Holy Spirit has talked to him, and his oneness with the Father. It's the summer of 1970. Another Moody Blues album comes out: *Question of Balance*. He will get it. This album is so right on for what is going on in the world that summer—in fact from the beginning of time. Freddy knows that this group of men are special.

Another year goes by. A friend of his, Jim, asks him to go on a long ride up north to help share the driving. He wants to see a girlfriend he thinks he is in love with. They leave about 7:00 a.m., and about seven hours into the ride, not even out of Florida yet, Jim lights up a joint. He asks if Freddy would like to try some pot.

Freddy has been against smoking anything all his life, but now at twenty-one, almost twenty-two, his thoughts for pot is changing. As the hours pass, he goes and he gets stoned. His first reaction is laughter, lots more laughter as the boys go merrily down the road, an enjoyable time had by all.

After returning from this road trip, he is hanging with another friend who smokes pot. On a Saturday afternoon, there sitting in his living room and just after taking the second hit from a friend, the thought in his head is that life is but a joke.

God put us here as a joke! He picks up his Bible, and when he looks at the words, he sees it with no problem—his dyslexia, gone. The marijuana has helped his reading problem. He opens the Bible to the book of Matthew and falls in love with God's word even more now, and he can read without any dyslexia problems. He can't stop reading the Bible now. All the love is magnified a thousand times just reading his Bible. He reads it every day with the Holy

Spirit guiding him and showing him the truth in God's word.

He is going to join the plumbing union and go to apprentice school in the summer. Brenda is working as a waitress. The parties are still on the weekends, and Freddy is still filming the guys. Another two years has passed. Vietnam is getting very bad, and the army draft is calling. Freddy's number is up again. Because of his first child, he does not have to go to the war. His wife is taking the pill, and they are not thinking, "Let's have another baby to stay out of the war." He gets a letter from the army saying in three months he should report to Miami for a physical. Now what is he going to do? The next month, Brinda gets tested, and she is two months with child. Freddy is deferred from the war. He thanks God in prayer. In seven months, his wife will have their second child. It will be another beautiful girl. It's February of 1973. She is born on the same day as the first daughter, three years apart. He knows they were both gifts from the Father so he would not have to go to the war. The Father has plans for him.

Brinda's father smokes two or three packs a day and drinks beer after each working day. He dies of a heart attack. The family is saddened. Freddy and Brinda move in with her mother to help her and her little brother. They both forget to make a change of address form for the mail, and when the letter from the pluming union is sent to him, he does not get it because of the change of address form was not made. The letter goes back to the union address unknown. He does not understand why the company he is working for does nothing when they put his name in, and they go to the union meetings each week. They knew each day Freddy was on the job working for them. There is so much building going on in south Florida. He leaves the plumbers, because he's not going to go to the apprentice program, and he joins the carpenters' labor union.

Months later, the family moves out of her mother's house and into a house across the street, a nice two-bedroom house with a carport. As a union man, he is working at the condo on the beach of Boca. This building he is working is forty stories. He takes his movie camera and makes a movie of the last day on this one—starting the first floor at this building and seeing all the other building being done in the cities from Fort Lauderdale to Boca on the beaches where he, and his friends would have party years earlier.

He is moved with sadness and thinks he understands how the American Indians felt when they lost everything. After several more months at work, the company makes him supervisor over the labors. That comes with a twenty cent increase per hour. He's making good money: $6.20 an hour. With both of them working, all is going good for the married couple. He's reading his Bible every day, because his dyslexia problem got fixed. He has gone thru the Bible cover to cover twice in one year. Reading through the delightful book. These are some of the scriptures that the Holy Spirit opens Freddy's mind to.

He thinks about his heavenly Father and how much he loves his children. Father, Son, and Holy Spirit are one, and we are one with him. He is within us believers. We are all connected. Freddy's desires to get closer to God, the feelings of oneness are getting stronger, he thinks about his youth miracles.

> For God has not given us the spirit of fear; but of power, and of love, and of a sound mind. Be not thou therefore ashamed of the testimony of our Lord, nor of me his prisoner; but be thou partakers of the afflictions of the gospel according to the power of God; Who has saved us, and called us with a holy calling, not according to our works, but according to his own purpose and grace, which was given us in Christ Jesus before the world began. But is now made manifest by the appearing of our Savior Jesus Christ, who has abolished death, and has brought life and immortality to light through the gospel: That good thing which

was committed unto thee keep by the Holy Spirit which dwelleth in us. (2 Timothy 1:7–10, 14)

Thou therefore, my son, be strong in the grace that is in Christ Jesus. Nevertheless, the foundation of God standeth sure, having this seal. The Lord knows them that are his. And, let everyone that names the name of Christ depart from iniquity. (2 Timothy 2:1, 19)

The word that came to Jeremiah concerning all the people of Judah in the fourth year of Jehoiakim the son of Josiah king of Judah, that was the first year of Nebuchadnezzar king of Babylon; The which Jeremiah the prophet spank unto all the people of Judah, and to all the inhabitants of Jerusalem, saying, "Therefore prophesy thou against them all these words, and say unto them, The Lord shall roar from on high, and utter his voice from his holy habitation; he shall mightily roar upon his habitation; he shall give a shout, as they that tread the grapes, against all the inhabitants of the earth. A noise shall come even to the ends of the earth; for the Lord has a controversy with the nations, he will plead with all flesh; he will give them that are wicked to the sword, saith the Lord.

Thus, saith the Lord of host, behold, evil shall go forth from nation to nation, and a great whirlwind shall be raised up from the coasts of the earth. And the slain of the Lord shall be at that day from one end of the earth even unto the other end of the earth: they shall not be lamented, neither gathered, nor buried; they shall be dung upon the ground. (Jeremiah 25:1, 30–33)

Behold, the days come, saith the Lord, that I will make a new covenant with the house of Israel, and the house of Judah: "But this shall be the covenant that I will make with the house of Israel; After those days saith the Lord, I will put my law in their inward parts, and write it in their hearts; and will be their God, and they shall be my people." And they shall teach no more every man his neighbor, and every man his brother, saying Know the Lord: for they shall all know me, from the least of them unto the greatest of them, saith the Lord: for I will forgive their iniquity, and I will remember their sin no more. (Jeremiah 31:31, 33–34)

To appoint unto them that mourn in Zion, to give unto them beauty for ashes, the oil of joy for morning, the garment of praise for the spirit of heaviness; that they might be called trees of righteousness, the planting of the Lord, that he might be glorified. For I the Lord love judgment, I hate robbery for burnt offering; and I will direct their work in truth, and I will make an everlasting covenant with them. For as the earth bringeth forth her bud, and as the garden causeth the things that are sown in it to spring forth; so, the Lord God will cause righteousness and praise to spring forth before all the nations. (Isaiah 61:3, 8, 11)

Now of the things which we have spoken this is the sum: We have such a high priest, who is set on the right hand of the throne of the majesty in the heavens; a minister of the sanctuary, and of the true tabernacle, which the Lord pitched, and not man.

But now has he obtained a more excellent ministry, by how much also he is the mediator of a better covenant, which was established upon better promises. (Hebrews 8:1, 2, 6).

But without faith it is impossible to please him: for he that cometh to God must believe that he is, and that he is a rewarder of them that diligently seek him. (Hebrews 11:6).

Freddy loves reading the Bible just as much as he loves the Moody Blues. Then it happens— the opening of the third eye.

# Chapter 4

## On a Threshold of a Dream

"When the white eagle of the north flies over head, and the browns, reds, and golds of autumn lie in the gutter dead, remember than the summer birds with wings of fire flaming, come to witness springs new hope, bourn of leaves decaying. As new life, will come through death, love will come with leaguer, love of love, and love of life, and giving without meager gives in return a wondrous yarn of a promise all most seen. Live hand in hand and together we will stand on a threshold of a Dream."

(Moody Blues)

One late evening, while Freddy is walking around the neighborhood, as he usually does twice a week. He's asking his heavenly Father about Jesus. He is questioning if Jesus is God, or is he just a prophet—just a man who just became really spiritual? Reading his Bible from cover to cover more than three times, he has had this on his mind. He has read in the Bible how Jesus and the Father are one, but he is in deep thought about it tonight. Something is driving this thought. "And he that sent me is with me: The Father has not left me alone; for I do always those things that please him" (John 8:29). "I and my Father are one" (John 19:30).

After about an hour of walking around, he quietly enters his house, and he walks to the back bedroom, and he sees all are sleeping. He gives everyone lightly on the forehead a good-night kiss. He loves his family, and he would like to be a great dad and good husband. He is too wide awake to sleep. Walking back to the living room, he sits on the floor in a yoga position in the dark and puts on headphones, which are plugged into his tape player. Not knowing what song will play, he just knows it would be one of the songs from the Moody Blues. He lowers his head and closes his eyes as if to pray and pushes the play button. The song starts with the sound of one string being plucked its middle C on a special sound instrument called a moong.

At that moment, in his mind between his eyes, a small dot of light appears. He hears notes go from C, D, E, F, G, A, B, to C. That's an octave. His eyes close. His head starts rising very slowly like on its own. Then all the notes blending together are making a big bang sound like on a piano. The little dot of light in his mind just grows brighter. The sound of the music makes his mind feel as if he is going up to heaven. The light in his mind is getting brighter and brighter, and brighter, as his head is rising. Then comes the words to the song as his mind is full of bright light.

"Be it sight, our sound, smell or touch, there is something inside that we need so much. The sight of the touch, the scent of the sound, or the strength of the Oak which roots deep into the ground, the wonder of flowers to be buried, and to burst up through tarmac too the sun again, or too fly to the sun without burning a wing, too lie in the meadow, and hear the grass sing, to have all these thing, and never resort to use them to help us to find, then laughter…"

The light in his mind is so bright it could not get any brighter. His mind is full of super bright light. He can even feel the light in his head, and that is forty seconds from start till end; he opens his eyes quickly. The light is gone. There is only darkness all around, no angel shining so brightly in front of him. It was in his mind. He takes off the headphones before the next song continues. His third eye is open; he is thrilled and scared at the same time. It feels like lightning is going through his veins. The Father of the universe has opened his mind through the music of the Moody Blues. He knows that this music is special. He is moved with the thought to open his Bible; he gets up from the floor, sits in a chair, as the darkness stirs. He opens the Bible at random: "Arise, shine; for thy light is come, and the glory of the Lord is raised upon you" (Isaiah 60:1).

"When the light comes in, there is no darkness, the light, Jesus said he is the light of the world" (John 9:5). He is shaken with a fear of all that just happened. He closes his Bible; the light made a strong impression. God has got his attention big-time. He's not looking to be a sounding voice, just thinking about his mind being enlightened. The words fill his head from one of the Moody Blues songs: "A beam of light will fill your head and you will remember what's been said; by all the good men this world has ever know." Is this the little book he has been reading, and memorizing all the heart melting, beautiful love thoughts? He falls into a light sleep on the recliner, then wakes up and goes to bed.

The next day at work, he's questions God, and the light, the total view. He knows that God has been with him from the beginning. He knows he's not special, but God does have a plan for his being here on earth, just like so many others believers, and his mind filled with light has got his attention. He is not telling anyone, that's for sure. His enlightenment, of the third eye, in his mind opening, he has too many questions. He tells no one! He has seen how people in the past who would speak out on their blessing is made fun of and laughed at, and only a few believed, but the ones who do want to make you out to be someone special, he's a sinner saved by God's grace like other believers, but he knows he is called for a mission, but what?

After a week, he calls the Moody Blues headquarters to ask about the song that gave him this light in his mind, has anyone called in about this happening? He would like to speak to one of the members of the group, Justin Hayward if possible. The girl on the line tells him, "No, we have not heard of this happing to anyone! And, no, you cannot speak to anyone of the group!" Then she hangs up.

It's Tuesday afternoon. At work, he hears the voice, in his right ear, "Seek me!" and again, "Seek me!" It's louder than a whisper. The Holy Spirit is answering his prayer from his evening walk: "Is Jesus God?" He has heard the voice before as a baby. "He's tricking you." Then baptize when he was twelve, the love and the bubble of love around him, no do not steal, and in his teens; become a preacher, and now in his early twenties, "Seek me. Seek me." "And it is impossible to please God without faith. Anyone who wants to come to him must believe that God exists and that he rewards those who sincerely seek him" (Hebrews 11:6).

He's not sure if he can leave. He has a pretty wife and two beautiful daughters born on the same day three years apart. Each one saves him from going to Vietnam, the day's work is done, and he is going home to the family.

The everyday family life is going on, and three weeks has passed. He is at work. It's Tuesday afternoon. He hears the voice, saying "Seek me!" He hears it through his right ear. Then, again, it says, "Seek me!" He knows he must, that this is the Holy Spirit talking! "Yes! Father, I will go."

"This is the purpose that is purposed upon the whole earth; and this is the hand that is stretched out upon all the nations. For the Lord of host has purposed, and who shall disannul it? and his hand is stretched out, and who shall turn it back" (Isaiah 14:26–27).

In the book of Luke, he has read the scripture where Jesus tells his disciples, "If you love father, mother, brother, sister, wife, son, or daughter, more they me you are not worthy to be my disciple…"

The light in his mind is surely an eye-opener. He would like to show the Father how much he loves him by doing his will; so he plans to leave the wife, and children, family, friends, and work without a word to anyone. If he tells anyone, he knows they would tell him he is nuts. He knows the Father is real, and calling.

He plans his sojourn, in search of the Christ of God, and the calling on his life at twenty-two. He knows he must go on a spiritual walk north till his search for God is over.

A month of family life has gone by. He is ready to go. It's Monday, 4:30 a.m., and everyone he knows, knows nothing of this sojourn. It's him and his heavenly Father. He has on a pair of shorts and a T-shirt and his leather sandals, which his sister in Hawaii made for him. He's not going to take any identification. His white sack with drawstrings is packed with two jars of soybeans wrapped in a beach towel. He has one pair of Levi's, and in the left-hand pocket is a dollar and fifty cents to buy milk to go with the soybeans, one bath towel, razor, toothbrush, toothpaste, in a little leather case, a bathing suit, one T-shirt, his Bible, and his little book inside his bible; but the last item to go into the bag is a beautiful white shirt with a pattern around the V-neck and the same pattern at the end of the puffy sleeves. He has not worn it yet. He received this beautiful shirt via mail from an unknown person, one month before his third eye was opened, with the bright white light that filled his mind. He leaves a note to his wife. It reads, "Brinda, I will call you sometime. I've got to go. Love, Frederick." There was no mention about the light or God.

He left his mother a note as well. It was dropped in a mailbox in the evening before the walk. The last thought from the little book reads,

Every year I live I am more
 convinced
That the waste of life lies in the
 love we have not given,
The powers we have not used,
The selfish prudence that will risk
 nothing, and which,
shirking pain, miss's happiness as
 well.
No one ever yet was the poorer in
 the long run,
for having once in a lifetime, let
 out all the length of all the reins.
(Dostoevsky)

The front door closes ever so silently. He is off walking in the dark, hungry and thirsting for more of God's light, his glory. He would like a Moses moment, a burning bush, some one on one with the Father of the universe.

"Glory you in his Holy name: let the heart of them rejoice that seek the Lord" (Psalm 105:3).

From his home, he walks to Dixie highway, about three blocks, then north to Sixty-Second

Street, another seven blocks, then east two miles to US Highway 1. Then he walks about three miles north, to Atlantic boulevard in Pompano, then east one mile to the beach. As he is stepping onto the sand, the light from the sun is rising, and the darkness is lifted, and the light is becoming the day. The clouds are light pink, very fluffy, with some light gray, with beams of bright orange as that big ball of light is rising at the end of the sea. He thinks back to California and all the sunsets. Has there ever been a more perfect sunrise? He sits on a picnic table and thinks there's no going back. He takes out the little book and reads the following verses out loud.

"'Love in your heart wasn't put there to stay. Love isn't love till you give it away' (Oscar Hammerstein; Psalm 51:1, John 13:34).

"'I want not only to be loved, but to be told I am loved, the realm of silence is large enough beyond the grave' (George Eliot; Ecclesiastes 9:10, 1 Timothy 6:7, and lots more).

"'Love is the coin with which we buy happiness in this life, and heaven in the next. But it is a coin with two sides. The reverse side is sacrifice, which is another word for the giving of ourselves' (Gilbert Hay, MSSST; Genesis 44:33, James 2:20).

"'The most important thing a Father can do for his children is to love their mother' (Theodore Hesburgh, CSC; Ephesians 5:25–33, John 12:26).'"

There are over one hundred thoughts in the little book. He has read this little book cover to cover seven times a day for the past year. Here it is, his first day of his spiritual walk going north in search of the Christ of God. Within less than ten minutes, he has thumbed through the little book; he has put every thought in his heart and mind. He eats the little book. It is as sweet as honey in his mouth, saying out loud the words, but it's bitter in his belly. In his heart, can you truly love like Jesus loves? This little book will do that to you when you read it. It's so sweet to read, how we should love one another, but this earthy thinking is sinking. We choose to hate first, and it's hard to love one other. We are so selfish as human beings. It's our sin nature.

Freddy does not know how important this little book really is, or how it fits into the future, but he loves reading the book because it fills his heart with love like Christ has done with his Holy Spirit.

His heart and mind are filled with the music of the Moody Blues: "A beam of light will fill you head and you'll remember what been said, by all the good men this world has ever know." The little book is full of good thoughts men have written, and he has remembered what they have said. The sojourn begins. "And I took the little book out of the angle's hand, and ate it up; and it was as sweet as honey in my mouth: and as soon as I eaten it, my belly was bitter" (Revelation 10:8–11).

The sandals come off his feet, cleaned, and he puts them into the white bag. Then he throws it over his shoulder. He starts his walk down to the water, and then as he puts his feet in, it's gets cooled at first, but gets nice as he starts walking north. The ocean is calm, and there is a light breeze. It's like "Itchycoo Park." It's all too beautiful. He has long hair down to his showers, but it's pulled back into a ponytail, and he has a mustache with a goatee. A hippie-looking young man soon to be twenty-three. He knows he must go around the inlet up ahead, as he walks up to the road walking north a couple of cars go by, then one car that passes him stops. A young fellow calls out, "Need a ride!" "Yes! Thanks!" He walks fast to catch up to the car. He gets in the backseat between two pretty girls, with a flower in their hair. With his white bag on his lap, they ask him where he is going.

In the late '60s through the '70s, people were out to help one another, love was in the music, love was in the air, love was all around the USA, and the light of love flowed out everywhere, even to other parts of the world. The driver asks again, "Where are you off to?" He tells them he's going back to his home in Philly. He really does not want to talk about his walk, searching for the Christ of God, and leaving his wife and kids. That is just too heavy on his mind right now. After a ten-minute ride going north, everyone is talking in the car, and he's thinking he is going to walk, and not ride when he started his sojourn. He wants to be a man of his word. They have driven over the inlet a mile back. He tells them to let him out here at this church not far from Hillsboro Beach Boulevard on the beach side A1A. They ask, "Are you sure you don't want to party with us!" "No, thanks," he says as he gets out. They are happy to help, and they wave goodbye to him.

"A good deed is never lost, he who sows courtesy, reaps friendship, and he who plants kindness gathers love." Basile, also read Luke 8:5, Matthew 13, Galatians 6:7–19, and Colossians 3:1–25.

He's about two blocks from the beach, so within three minutes, he is back on the beach with peace of mind, just him and the Lord. No one asking him questions, talking about things he will forget in an hour from now.

He just wants to know if Jesus is God or man? What does this light in his mind mean? What is his mission in this world? What is God calling him to do? It's so peaceful walking the beach with the ocean breeze, the sand at your feet, watching the aqua blue water, as the wave slowly coming on shore. He thinks of Daytona Beach, his destination for now.

The words of all the songs of the Moody Blues were so beautifully written, and the music put him in a peaceful state of mind. It was like it was made just for his ears only. He has fallen in deep love with the Moody Blues's words and music. He has bought each album after he heard that forth album at the party. There were six so far, the seventh due out this December, but he does not know where he will be at that day and time. He is searching for the truth in Christ Jesus. Was Jesus God on earth? He has read it in the Bible, but is the Bible true? Is it God's Word? After walking a good three hours, he rests. In his mind, he sings the song from the fifth album of the Moody Blues *Question of Balance*. It's the last song on the album.

The balance:

> After he had journeyed, and his feet were sour, he was tired he came unto and orange grove and he rested. And he lay in the cool, and

while he rested, he took to himself an orange and tasted it, and it was good, and he felt the earth to his spine and asked, and he saw the leaves above him, and the stars, and the vanes in the leaves, and the light, and the balance, and he saw magnificence perfection. Where on, he thought of himself in balance, and he knew he was. Just open your eyes and realize the way it's always been. Just open your mind to the way it's always been, just open your heart, and that's a start, and he thought of those he angered for he was not a violent man, and he thought of those he hurt, for he was not a cruel man, and he thought of those he frighten, for he was not and evil man, and he understood, he understood himself. Upon this he saw that when he was of anger or new hurt are felt fear, it was

because he was without understanding. And he learned compassion, and with his eye of compassion he saw his enmities like unto
himself. And he learned love, and
then he was answered.

After the daydream, he starts his walk again.
There is no going back. He's going to find out
who Jesus is: is he God or man, or God man?
The Holy Spirit must tell him. He would like
to see his burning bush, his one to one with the
Father.

He reaches Delray Beach at about three in
the afternoon. There is a little store on the other
side of the road. He goes across the road, buys a
pint of milk, goes back to the beach, and sits on
the sand. He's asking God to show him his glory
and fill him with his powerful love.

He opens the jar of soybeans, you can hear
the vacuum seal when opened, he eats his soybeans one by one, they must last for seven days
or longer. As he is soaking up the beauty, looking out to sea; thinking of God's love and how

happy all will be, when we all believe in Yasha, the Christ.

He is done eating, and thirty minutes has gone by, and a pretty, young girl walks up to him. She says, "Hi, my name is Rebecka." Then she starts to ask him some questions about God and heaven. Her head is blocking out the shining sun. The light shines about her head with a glow, like she is an angel. He invites her to sit down. They have been into a heavy spiritual conversation as the minutes turn into an hour. He then tells her he is on a sojourn to find the truth: was Jesus God on earth? That's what she believes, but he has seen a light in his mind and has heard the Holy Spirit. He knows the Father is calling. Rebecka tells him she needs to find her sister Leah. Rebecka looks him in the eyes. "I will be back. Stay here!" He tells her, "Do what you must do." She walks away. He lies back on the beach towel. The waves put him into a site sleep as the sun is slowly going down in the west.

He is shaken, and two girls are waking him up. What a cute pair of sisters, they would make a beautiful pair of book ends, but shakes that thought out of his mind. He must keep his focus on God and the truth of Christ Jesus. After about twenty minutes of talk, they ask him, "Where are you sleeping tonight?" He answered, "Somewhere on the beach." The girls tell him that their grandparents would not mind him sleeping in their house for the night. They're real nice people, and they live not far from where they are. They push the fact that it would be okay over and over. So he goes with them. They walk and talk for about half an hour or so, and Freddy is wondering where the girls live. It's been a long walk on A1A, but this is his first night out, and they are still walking north. He likes the thought of sleeping inside on the first night of the walk, to finding out who Jesus is. God or just a man and what is his calling why has God called him? This is foremost on his mind, and having the light fills his mind, all he wants is for the Father of the universe to show him his glory and tell him who the Christ of God is, and he wants to know what this enlightenment means. After turning west and going over a little bridge that goes over the intercostals, then reaching a little road going north walking for five minutes as the sun is setting, on his first day of his sojourn, they are a block away. The girls tell him that the grandparents will not be home tonight. They are sorry they lied but wants him to stay with them tonight. As they walk up to the house, he thinks they are afraid of being alone, and that while the old folks are gone, they need a man in the house. Rebecka opens the door, and Leah goes in first, then Freddy follows, and Rebecka closes the door but does not lock it.

It's only a one-bedroom house with one bath and a little living room, and they sit at the small kitchen table for four and talk about dinner. He tells them he's only eating soybeans while on his spiritual walk but a drink would be nice. The girls giggle and say they are eating only peanuts! He asks if he can read from the Bible. They say, "Sure."

"Peace be to this house the harvest truly is great, but the laborers are few: pray ye therefore the Lord of the harvest, that he would send forth laborers into his harvest. And in the same house remain, eating and drinking such things as they give: for the laborer is worthy of his hire. The kingdom of God is come nigh unto you" (Luke 10:2-9).

He opens his jar of soybeans. They bring out their peanuts in a big bag. All of them laugh over the fact that they are having a "nut fast." Even throw soybeans are not a nut. After eating and drinking a glass of milk together, the girls turn on the record player and put on album called God *Spell.* He tells them he has never heard of this record. They tell him it's from a Play God Spell it's like the Play Jesus Christ Super Star. After hearing two songs, there is a knock on the door. Then it opens, and a man comes in. He's in his late twenties. He is a hippy-looking guy, and it looks like he has not showered in days, and he is drunk and high, which makes him look like he has a disability. The girls say hi to Bob. He starts talking loud and being very disrespectful to them. The three are talking about spiritual things, which the girls love to hear, but Bob is being very disrespectful in his speech even though they try to be nice to him, but he is too high or on LSD. The music is playing in the background. The young girls ask him to leave, and Freddy stands up, and he is a good foot taller than the high hippy and tells him it would be the right thing to do, unless you would like to hear the word of the Lord and study the Bible with them. The door is opened, and he stumbles himself out. The girls lock the door behind him. They thank Freddy for his help and sit down and hear another song. Rebecka asks Freddy if he would like to take a shower. He says, "Yes! That would be nice." So he walks around the corner to the bathroom. Boy! Showers are refreshing. He feels refreshed after walking all day on the beach. When he comes back, Rebecka and Leah leave the room to clean up themselves and take a shower. He thanks the Lord for a place to shower and sleep for the first night out. Then he opens his Bible and starts reading. Thirty minutes have gone by, and he hears the girls walk out from the back room to the living room. He stops reading, and he looks up at them. The girls have smiles on their faces and dressed in see-though lingerie, and they are standing before him. Leah is in red, and Rebecka in black. Their pleasant sweet fragrance coming from their almost-naked bodies fills the room. The fruit looking oh-so beautiful and wanting to be pluck. Rebecka asks if she could have sex with him first, then my sister.

He is taken by surprise. He thanks Rebecka and Leah for their sweet, lovely thoughtfulness, but he is on a spiritual walk, not an earthly one. This is not what he is looking for. His mind has been opened. He has seen a great light. Nothing on earth can keep him from being one with God. He thanks them for their kindness. Then Rebecka asks if she can at lease lie next to him through the night. He tells her they can sleep head to head on the living room floor, but not side to side. Leah goes to the bedroom, and Freddy and Rebecka sleep on the floor the top of their heads, touching heads.

In the early morning, he wakes up first. Their heads are still touching. They were like that all night long. He goes to the bathroom to make ready for his walk. When he comes out, the girls who are still in their lingerie are sitting at the kitchen table. They hand him a glass of orange juice. He drinks it down fast. He thanks them for their hospitality. The girls give him a kiss on the lips. He turns and walks out the door into the first light of the second day.

"If any man will come after me, let him deny himself, and take up his cross daily, and follow me. For whosoever will save his life shall lose it: but whosoever will lose his life for my sake, the same shall save it" (Luke 9:23-24).

The house was not far from highway US 1. He takes it first walking north on the sidewalk. For about three miles, there are little hotels on both sides of the highway. The morning walk with a nice breeze as Mr. Sun is just working his way up. Walking on the beach was sweet, but walking in sandals on the hard sidewalk, then on the grass and dirt on the side of the road with cars passing by bites! After hours of walking, he comes to the road that takes you to the bridge to go over the intercostal to get to the beach. As he is walking onto the bridge that goes over the intercostals waterway, he smells the ocean. His feet can't wait till they hit the sand, and the eyes see the aqua blue ocean. As he gets to the beach, he takes a rest on the sand and opens his Bible somewhere in the New Testament and reads two lines, "So likewise, whosoever he be of you that forsake not all that he has, he cannot be my disciple."

Then he reads in Romans where Paul is writing how Abraham when he believed God he counted it for righteousness. This builds up his faith. He is doing the right thing, seeking the Lord first and his righteousness.

Then he brings out his little book and reads.

"Love is the coin with which we buy happiness in this life, and heaven in the next, but love is a coin with two sides. The reverse side is sacrifice, which is another word for the giving of ourselves" (Gilbert Hay, MSSST).

He reads the little book cover to cover again. He has memorized each one. His heart is filled with Christ's love knowing only Jesus could love like this. He thanks the Lord for his eyes to see the beauty all around and his mind to understand his word and the love and the joy unspeakable. He truly believes God is going to show him miracles and signs of his power. He would like a Jacob moment, to wrestle with God.

Freddy gets up, shakes off the sand from his beach towel, wraps the two jars of soybeans, puts it in his bag, and starts walking north, with his feet in the cool ocean water, walking on the beautiful Florida beaches. If he sees any dead animal—bird, fish, crabs—he would take the time to bury them with a prayer. The beach property—there are not many condos, just homes here and there—is mostly woods on the west side of the beach. The morning being cool and breezy time goes by quick. As Tuesday afternoon sun is getting hot, he is getting into the area called millionaires row the beaches are private beaches. The homes are off the beach on the other side of A1A, but they think the beach is theirs. This is where John Lennon of the Beatles has his mansion on the road facing the beach. He sings the song "Tuesday Afternoon." "Tuesday afternoon I'm just beginning to see now I'm on my way it does not matter to me chasing the clouds away, something is calling to me the trees are drawing me near I've got to find out why the gentle voices I hear explaining only the sigh" Moody Blues:

He is walking in the small ocean waves, thinking of God and mostly asking for a sign that maybe he can tell him why he is called.

Up ahead on the roadway, he sees two policemen waving for him to come up to the road. As he reaches them, he says, "Yes, Officers!" One grabs his bag. The other grabs Freddy like he just killed someone. They walk across the road. Freddy is pushed to the car and told, "Spread your hands and feet." Then one dumps the white bag on the hood. His Bible comes out first, and they check everything for drugs. Then the officer puts the items back in the sack, and not in an enjoyable way. Then they put him in the backseat and drive him to a small station. There they check him out in more detail, looking up his name in the database. He has no ID, so he tells them his real name, but he tells them that back in Fort Lauderdale he lost his wallet and suitcase, and now everything in his bag is all that he has left and that he is walking back to

Philly. Another hour goes by; they cannot find anything bad on him, so they give him a ride out of West Palm Beach. They go over the inlet bridge, and now they are in North Palm Beach. They stop and let him out. "See ya kid. Good luck getting back home."

That is the best thing that could have happened. He does not know about the West Palm Beach Inlet. He would have walked miles out of his way if he had kept on walking on the beach to the inlet, then turn and walk back for ten miles to where there is a bridge to get across the inlet. The police saves him miles of walking. It would have been over four hours of wasted time, even though he is in no hurry. The police help him greatly, angels unawares. "They are godsent. Thank you, Lord Jesus!"

Freddy is walking on sidewalks on A1A for about half an hour, then on the grassy weeds and dirt. Then he gets to where a road that leads to the beach. It's North Juno Beach. He passes the Seminole Golf Club, which has a gated entranceway. Only millionaires can play on this course. He keeps on walking and comes to a church on the beach side. It's a good place to sleep. He's not sure what is up ahead, and it looks very safe for the night. He keeps asking the Lord for a vision, a word, or a dream for enlightenment so he can open the mind again and see his glory. The stars in the sky twinkle, and in the distance, the ocean waves put him to sleep. With all that walking, he is sound asleep.

He wakes up just before the dawn of a new day, the third of his sojourn. He thanks the Lord and reads the little book from cover to cover. He opens his Bible. He reads Matthew 7 where it says, "Do not judge, get the beam out of my eye first, then I can help my brother, then make sure you understand like Jesus with Love and grace, and compassion." He eats a handful of soybeans, drinks water from a water outlet on the side of the church, brushes his teeth, throws water on his face, and pats his face with the beach towel.

With the love of the Lord in his heart, he starts his walk, walking on Juno Beach. Then miles north, he comes up to another inlet and goes over the Jupiter Inlet Bridge. The water was so blue you had to look at the color, and just say awesome! The inlet breeze cools him off. He passes Carlin Park, and the next light a right-hand turn can get him to the beach, but he's not sure if he can even walk on it, because the very rich own it. Plus, the next inlet coming up, would he have to walk back to this road? He does not know, so he walks on US1 for now, and there are no sidewalks, just woods on either side. He's just on the side of the road walking in grass and dirt. his feet are getting sore, not like soft sand and cool water on the feet. He passes Jonathan Dickerson State Park on the west side of the road. He has camped out there, before he got married. As the morning turns into afternoon, he goes through small older-looking towns like Hope Sound. Then he arrives at Stuart, walks east on SE Ocean Boulevard for about a mile, then across the canal bridge, and, finally, he is very happy to get back on the beach. It was so empty and so quiet. There are no cars. The music of the Moody Blues comes up in his mind with the breeze.

"Throw the eyes of a child you will come out and see that your world is spinning round and throw life you will be a small part of a hope of a love that excise, throw the eyes of a child you will see" (Moody Blues).

Off with his sandals, he let his feet hit the sand, stepping into the water going north. His feet are happy again, walking in the cool water. Mr. Lovely Beautiful Day is in front of him time passes, and he must go back to the highway over the bridge on Seaway Drive to US1 to the next bridge N. Causeway and back on the beach in Fort Pierce. He walks north along Vero Beach, then to Melbourne, and he feels like time is nonexistent. With a clear mind as he's going through Coco Beach, the Holy Spirit puts a thought into his head, which stops him still: "You must get to Daytona before sunset." He starts thinking he knows if he continues to walk he will get there, but way after dark, plus another inlet up ahead he does not know about. By car, it would take a good hour at fifty-five miles per hour with no red lights. He makes his way up the soft white sand to the highway. He gets his sandals out of his bag, cleans his feet and slips them on, and crosses the road to get water to drink at the gas station. Out of nowhere, a very old man walks up to him and asks, "Do you have any spare change?" Where does this man come from? There was no one around; then, *pop*, this man is standing next to him? Without any hesitation, Freddy, with lots of love in his heart, says, "Sure, old man," and gives him his last fifty cents. He tells the old man, "You need it more than I do. God bless you." The old man didn't know that was his last fifty cents; only the Father knows. He turns to go to the gas station. He turns his head to see the old man, but he is gone already. "Giving without measure gives in return a wondrous yearn, live hand in hand and together we will stand on the threshold of a dream" (Moody Blues).

He approaches the gas station where there is an outside water fountain. He gets a long cool drink. He walks back to the road, then crosses the street to get back on the beach side. He steps onto the sidewalk and takes his sandals off to walk down to the water. A car stops with three guys, and they yell to tell Freddy, "We're going to Daytona Beach. Do you need a ride?" Freddy looks back to where the old man asks him for the money, and in his heart, he thanks God, and he gets into the car; it is another test.

It's a test from the Father. Everything we do is a test. How will we act in each circumstance of life? When the Holy Spirit tells you something is going to happen, it's going to happen! The guys have already started to party as they drive away. One asks Freddy, "How about a hit of pot?" "No, thank you." He tells them he is on a spiritual walk, searching for the Christ of God. They all say, "That's cool, man!" As they drink their beers, they all ramble on with words of this and that.

Before long, they are in South Daytona Beach, then in Famous Daytona Beach. As Freddy is getting out of the car, he thanks them with a thought. "A good deed is never lost, he who sows courtesy, reaps friendship, and he who plants kindness gathers love." They are lost for words and look at each other. Then he said, "God has blessed me. You are my blessing. Thank you again."

He turns around and walks to the beach, sits down on the soft white sand just thinking how great is God, how he works in our life, Freddy believes here in this city tonight God will answer his questions. He prays, "Show me your glory tonight, Lord. Let me see you. Thank you, amen."

In about two hours, the sun will have set. He walks to the ocean for a swim. He hits the water headfirst. It wakes him up. He swims a couple of laps north and south, then body surfs into the shore. The waves are bigger there. He then walks to the showers that are on the beach, by the entrance and exits ramps, where the cars enter the beach. Yes! The cars are driven on the beach. He turns on the water and stands under it for five minutes. Then after a good wash, he goes to the public restroom where he shaves off his three-day beard. Then he takes off his bathing suit, quickly dries off, and puts on a pair of blue jeans, then his white spiritual shirt, and lets down his long hair. Leaving that area, he finds a good place to hide his bag, along the seawall of a hotel. It's dark, and no one around. He walks around the boardwalk. He has no money. After about an hour of sightseeing, he goes to the end of boardwalk and walks down a street. He passes one store, looks at the people, then the next store. As his head turns to look in the store's front window, he looks right into the eyes of a young girl who's in the back with a customer. Their eyes lock in on each other. He cannot take his eyes off her eyes, and she does the same. They just stare at each other. This powerful feeling of love or a force so strong has entered them. A good minute or two has gone by, and he breaks the stare. "Oh! Lord Jesus!" He walks away, and he thinks about what just happened, that powerful energy he felt. He's driven to go back to the store. He goes in to see the girl and asks if she felt the same feeling, but when he goes in the store, the girl is waiting on that same person but looks at him and gives him a smile. So he walks around and looks at seashells. After seven minutes, which seemed forever to him, she works her way over to Freddy and, in a lovely soft voice, said, "Hi, my name is Sarah." She then whispered, "My boss is here! Let me show you the items over here." They walk over to the end of the store. She whispers, "We can talk here." He asks, "Did you feel a strong energy force when our eyes met?"

She said, "Yes! I must tell you my heart was pounding very fast. What would you like to do about us? I get off at 10:15. How about you meet me back here then?" He looks her in the eyes and tells her, "I will return at your request." She smiles with her green eyes. He picks up her hand and gives it a soft kiss. He walks out of the store and does not look back. It's around 8:45. He walks to the beach and sits on the seawall. He prays, "Father, thank you that you hear me. I would like to know what to do. I know I'm not here to fall in love with another girl. I have a wife and children. This energy I felt with Sarah was so strong it must mean something. I thank you for Sarah. Bless my family, and help me see your light, your glory tonight. Amen." He sits there, hearing the waves, looking out into the sea of darkness, with so much more going through his mind as the time slowly drifts by.

It's 10:15 p.m. He's standing outside the shop. Sarah and her boss walk out, and he locks the front door, and she floats over to what she hopes will blossom into love. The boss asks Sarah, "Are you going to be all right?" She tells him, "Yes! He is my friend!" As they walk away, he tells her his dilemma: he has no car and no money, and he has been eating only soybeans for the last three days. She tells him, "I have a car. I have money. I'm here for you." They walk to Mc D's down the block. As they walk, she tells him, "I'm in my first year of college, and by the way, I am Jewish!" He tells her, "That's beautiful," and he likes her even more. As they get to Mc D's, he tells her he does not eat meat. He gets an outside table while she goes inside. It's not very busy, and within minutes, they are both eating french fries and sharing a soda pop. As minutes become an hour, he tells her he is searching for the Christ of God. She is fascinated with the young hippy-looking guy. Sarah is asking him out for lunch tomorrow before she goes to work. She has no class tomorrow morning. *This is all* God's *timing*, he is thinking. He needs a healthy meal if he is going to keep walking north. "Okay, that would be nice," she said. "We will eat at the Chinese restaurant here on this road, and they part with a gentle kiss on the lips." She drives off, and he walks back to the beach.

He walks back to where he hides his white bag with his things down onto the soft white sand. He takes off his clothes, puts on a T-shirt and shorts, lays out his beach towel, and uses the bag as a pillow, just like he has done the last two nights. and how blessed he was on the first night taking a shower, and thankful he had a shower here on the beach cold, but a shower. There is a feeling only a shower can bring cleansing to the body and mind a clean feeling.

He's asking the Father of the universe to give him a word, with his voice, because he knows in his heart he is not here to fall in love with a sweet young beautiful Jewish girl, like Sarah, but he is just human, and a man, and love is so grand when it works hand in hand. It is low tide, and the waves are small, and the sound of the waves, and with a soft breeze slowly puts the sojourner to sleep.

Morning has broken, and he is awake but cannot remember his dream, no burning bush, not a word, just a good night's rest. It will be a half hour before sunrise, and he finishes his meditation, praying to the Father. He takes a walk down to the pier and back on the hard sand. Then he dives into the water for a morning wake-up swim back to his beach towel area. He lies on the towel and is warmed by the rising sun. On this day, he must face the difficulty of telling Sarah he must move on. It's been four days, and there is still no burning bush, but God has shown his hand and the tests he is going through. He's been eating soybeans for four days, and he needs a healthy meal if he is going to keep walking north. He is to meet her at a Chinese restaurant near the pier by eleven thirty. He has time to kill. He reads his little book. "The world is a great mirror. It reflexes back to you what you are, if you are loving, friendly, and helpful the world will prove loving, and friendly, and helpful to you. The world is what you are" (Thomas Dreier). Be like Christ, but if Christ was God, it would be easy for him to be himself. We are not God but only human, and it's not that simple.

He reads his Bible. "A new heart also will I give you, and a new spirit will I put within you: and I will take away the stony heart out of your flash, and I will give you an heart of flash. And I will put my Spirit within you, and cause you to walk in my statutes, and you shall keep my judgments, and do them. And you shall dwell in the land that I gave too your fathers; and you shall be my people, and I will be your God" (Ezekiel 36:26–28). There is too much on his mind—God, his family, and now Sarah. The morning goes by slow. He takes a walk around the boardwalk. It was big back when he was twelve, and memories come back being here with the friends he had. They would pick up soda bottles and get the deposit, play the games, make the IBTC club, and say they would be friends forever. Now he sees the light, and decides to be more like Christ, for God, and not find a new lover.

Time has come, and he walks to the restaurant and sees Sarah; she is even prettier in the light. She is as beautiful as the day. They get a table in the back to be away from the lunch crowd. Talking for half an hour, she asks him how soon he can move up to Daytona. There is lots of work up here. His heart is melting as he is looking at her pretty face. She is as sweet as chocolate, and he is slowly being pulled into her little dream—just like how Eve pulled Adam into eating from the tree of the knowledge of good and evil. While they eat lunch, her conversation is sounding better all the time. He's getting along well with her. When they are done with lunch sipping tea, she asks, "Would you like some ice cream from a store on the boardwalk? I like to visit on my breaks." He loves ice cream, and the bill in a little dish is laid on the table. She puts her hard-working money in the dish, and they walk to the board walk holding hands till they get to the place where good ice cream is made.

FREDERICK F. HAUSSMAN JR.

As they leave the shop licking the ice cream cone, they walk over to the railing seeing out over the beach. Sarah is into the sea of love, and Freddy starts thinking how to tell her it is over before it starts. He would like God to step in and give him some courage. The love feeling is great, but he knows he must focus on God. As they walk round the boardwalk, she lets him know she is loving him. Then Sarah looks at her watch and says, "Let's start walking to my workplace," as they come to a street, where there is water in the road only one way over, they must walk through the water. She looks at him with her eyes, as if to say, "Pick me up in your strong arms. Carry me over the water, my Knight, my love." The Spirit puts the opportunity to fall from grace in his mind. He does nothing to help her walk over the water. She is very upset. He begins to tell her he is searching for the Christ of God: is Jesus God? He wants to find out his mission on earth. His mind is full of light before he takes his walk. "Sarah! This love is not real. It's a test from God to see what I will do. I cannot be with you. I'm very sorry.

162

She walks away mad, and off she goes to work. They will not see each other again. He knows the love is real for a moment in time when they locked eyes, but God knows he needs the food, and it is in God's plans from the beginning, the test. Will he leave his wife and children for a new earthly love? No! He will not. The love for God is so much more! But the body needs food, and God arranges it.

He's at the beach and hears on the radio of a big gathering of Jewish teachers in Jacksonville ninety miles up the beach, and he is moved by the Holy Spirit go to the meeting and tell them about Christ's love. He knows he has the Holy Spirit in him, but he does not know Jesus, if he is God or man, but he has experienced his great love and light. He should know so he can tell others of this love he has gotten from the Father.

He must make a choice: go on with faith or go home. He decides to go home and be the man and the father for his girls. He has been blessed on this walk of faith, and God has counted it for righteousness. "And the Lord said unto Moses, I will do this thing also that thou has spoken; for thou has found grace in my sight, and I know thee by name" (Exodus 33:17).

He calls his wife. "Yes! I'm all right. I'm in Daytona Beach. Can you please send the money to the Western Union office in Daytona Beach? I need to get a room for the night and clean up. I'll be home Saturday night some time. I'll start hitchhiking in the morning. I'll be home on Saturday night for sure. Thank you. See you soon, love you." He knows Sunday will be their third wedding anniversary. He wants his marriage to work, to be a great dad for his girls, and to be a good husband. He knows God loves him. Whatever he decides to do, the Father gives us free will. He never stops loving us because of his grace through Christ.

The Western Union office is over the bridge, so he walks, and when he gets there, the money is not in yet. So he walks to a big church on the corner, thinking maybe God's glory will be in there. He also decides to sit in the air conditioner and read the Bible while waiting. It could be over two hours of waiting time. He reads the Bible. "Before I formed thee in the belly I

SEVENTH MESSENGER

knew you; and before thou came forth out of the womb I sanctified you, and I ordained you a prophet unto the nations" (Jeremiah 1:5). For about thirty minutes inside this very big quite peaceful church, he was sitting in the last pew away from the front door when several teenage girls come in the church started talking. Freddy sees them first and keeps his head in the book to show he's not interested in them. The girls walk to the back as a group. Then one walks up closer to Freddy, and she wants to find out what's he is doing in our church. She says, "Hi, my name is Sunny Day!" He stops reading and looks up into the prettiest blue eyes of a young girl. She walks up to him even closer. Both of them lock eyes, and she asks some questions; and he looks at her lovely smile, pretty face, blond hair, and nice finger, and she's drawing him in. Then she invites him to a Saturday picnic with the youth ministry. She tells him, "I'll keep you company. Please come. It will be fun!" Would he like to spend more time with Miss Sunny Day? Only a person on a spiritual walk would say no. He looks at the Bible, and he knows it's just another

165

test. He tells her how nice it all sounds but he must be home this weekend. He sits back down and reads the Bible, and Miss Sunny Day leaves with her friends. He reads for another hour. He's reading John 14: this is where Jesus is telling his disciples; he is the only way to the Father. He loves the book of John. It's been over two hours, and he walks to the Western Union office. The money is in, and he signs the paperwork and gets his thirty-five dollars. He walks back to the beach, gets a room, takes a long shower, dries off, then falls on the bed, praying for a vision—an Exodus 33 moment, like Moses had, where he could not see God's face, only his back profile. He then falls into a deep sleep. You don't know what a good bed is till you lose it. After hours of sleeping, he gets up and takes a shower again. At about 6:30 p.m., he gets a bite to eat. As the darkness draws on and the meal is over, he walks around the boardwalk one last time, looking at all the people the ones in love. He is hitchhiking in the morning back to Fort Lauderdale, but he's hoping God does something to change his mind tonight in the hotel room. Maybe that's what will happen. He prays on his knees, then in bed for a good-night's sleep. He is thinking maybe a dream will come. He's "on a threshold of a dream." He is up before the sun, and he takes another shower to wake up. Then he has the small box of cereal, which he bought with a pint of milk, and he eats quickly.

He's packed, ready to walk to I95. Mr. Sun has already popped up his head. He doesn't know how long it will take to get to I95 out west or to get back home to Fort Lauderdale, but he has a stronger faith in God. He's ready to tell his wife he will be the man for her and the best dad ever for the girls. He reaches the south ramp of I95 about nine o'clock in the morning. It takes two hours to get here, and there is a young man at the north ramp. He tells Freddy he's been here for over forty-five minutes. Freddy tells him, "You have got to have faith." He puts out his thumb, and the first car stops. The young man yells, "How do I get faith?" Freddy yells, "Ask God!" As he walks fast up to the car waiting, he opens the door and gets in. The driver said, "Hello, my name is Samul." "Hello, my name is Fred. Nice to meet you. Thank you for the ride." The middle-aged man tells him he's going to Boca Raton. That is a four-hour ride from Daytona. Not bad for a first ride, with small talk for about an hour and a half, then quiet time. After I95 ends, Samul stops at a store. He buys Freddy a beer and a sandwich. He gets some for himself too. Freddy looks thin. He thanks Samul and thinks about the good in man. When they get to Boca, Freddy gets out of the car and thanks Samul again. Not more than ten seconds after, another guy yells, "Need a ride?" He is in a nice truck, and Freddy gets in and drives him to Pompano Beach, and as he gets out of that ride, he is picked up and driven to Fort Lauderdale's Sixty-Second Street, the street he walked down six days ago. He is now two miles from home. Only five hours ago, he was in Daytona Beach. He knows this is god-sent. He thanks the Father over and over as he walks west, but it's not over. As he is walking a car, and not just an ordinary car, a new beautiful red Mustang stops up ahead. He walks up to the window of the car and looks right into the eyes of a beautiful Playboy girl who looks like a player, and she says in a lovely voice, "Need a ride?" He gets in, and she drives off. She talks first, asking him, "Where are you going?' He tells her home from a long walk. She asks him if he likes to party. He tells her, "Oh yes!" She tells him, "I just got off from work. Would you like to party with me tonight?" He looks at her, and he sees the perfect sex toy—green eyes, jet-black hair, with a super body, cool car. She was hot to trot. Then he has a flashback of the girls who came to him in the last five days on his spiritual walk. It is another test, and this one is very, very hot. He tells her, "Sorry, but I must get home. Thanks for the ride. You can let me out here." She stops, and he starts to get out, she asks, "I'll take you to your house!" "No, thank you. I've got to get out here. Thank you." That's all he needs—for this beautiful girl to drop him off at the house. Brinda will not believe he walked to Daytona Beach. He looks into her eyes, and he says, "A good deed is never lost; he or she who sows curtsey reaps friendship he who plants kindness gathers love" (Basile).

He gets out of the car and thanks her again. In his mind, he wants to make his marriage work. He walks another three blocks up to his home; he opens the door that he had closed behind him on his quest for God's burning bush: Who am I? What's my lot in life? No one is home. No one thought he would make the sojourn back in just six hours. That was a miracle! He lies down on the sofa thanking God for all the rides that brought him home fast and safe, but he is a little disappointed because he did not get a burning bush; then he falls into a deep sleep.

He wakes up to his three-year-old daughter giving him a big hug. He jumps up, and she is still hugging around his neck. He has a nice bond with his first daughter. Then he kisses the six-month-old baby and his wife. She is not happy at all. After they put the girls to bed, they walk outside to talk. Freddy tells her he will be the best husband a woman can have, but he asks her one thing: for her to stop smoking cigarettes. Brinda just gets into his face with the words "Fuck you! Who do you think you are, you son of a bitch!" She goes on, and on, and on with negative words in his face, just like her mother did to her dad and brothers. He knew this will not work, and he sleeps on the sofa that night. The next morning, Freddy takes a drive to nowhere. In his mind, he's saying, "God, I did not get my question answered during my sojourn. I know you were with me, because I got home early, and the last ride I had with that beautiful girl that just wanted to party with me, on top of my time together with all of the other girls that showed me love was all a test. But who is Jesus?" That very second, the Holy Spirit rushes into his heart with a love that was so pure, so strong, so wonderful, bursting fourth with the power from on high; and he starts to cry. His heart is filled with a love so strong he can't stop crying. The love is getting even stronger. He must pull the van over. With the flow of love energy that poured into his heart and the power of the love of the Father, the tears flowed out, and his heart is filled of joy, and he is the happiest at that moment. The love is a thousand times stronger than the love that came over him after he got baptized. The best love ever this was pure love. This was the power of the Father's Holy Spirit. Then, in his mind, he hears a very loud, "Yes! You can take it to the bank. Jesus is God in the flash."

"And you are Christ's; and Christ is God's" (1 Corinthians 3:23).

The love was so great he keeps crying, and he thanks the Lord of lords; Jesus is the Christ of God. The love pouring through his heart finally has subsided. He wipes the tears from his face with his T-shirt, thanking God over and over.

This is his burning bush moment. He didn't see his glory but got the love. This is powerful. Having too much of this love, your heart would burst, a joy unspeakable. The Father lets Freddy know how great and real he is, but he will keep his relationship between him and the Father low-key and gets back on the road praising Jesus.

He moves out of the house knowing he cannot live with Brinda, who told him he was a fool to seek God, but he is not done with his spiritual education. He checks into a one-room apartment. He still has his job. He was such a good worker. The company does not fire him because he only lost five days. Now he makes plans for a forty-day fast in the woods at Jonathan Dickerson State Park in Jupiter Florida. He passed by it on his walk to Daytona Beach. It's September, and he sets his eye on December 1 till January 9—forty days of fasting.

In the meantime, he sees his children on the weekends but does not mention to anyone he is going on another journey. This time, he's longing for more of Christ's love but also his calling. He wants to be loved again by Christ nonstop. He studies his Bible every night. No more parties, no drinking, and no smoking pot. His mind is focused on the Father. He reads John 6:37: "All that my Father giveth me shall come to me; and him that cometh to me I will in no wise cast out" (John 6:65). "Therefore said I unto you, that no man can come unto me, except it was given unto him of my Father. We do not pick Jesus; The Father picks you to know Jesus. The Holy Spirit glides you as you read his word, and the Spirit is moving Freddy to understand the living word of God. And

without controversy great is the mystery of godliness: God was manifest in the flesh, justified
in the Spirit, seen of angels, preached unto the
Gentiles, believed on in the world, received up
into glory" (1 Timothy 3:16).

He loves the Moody Blues and hears their
music each day. The seventh album will be out
in December, but he will not be around any
store to buy it. He tells a few of his friends of
his second sojourn coming up. Behind his back,
they are saying, "Who does he think he is?"

September, October, November, the
moment is here. Time to give up all earthly pos-
sessions. He drops off his clothes and only keeps
a few. All he has can fit in the VW. He has his
camping gear, tent, lantern, ice chest, gas stove
to boil water, sleeping bag, some blankets, pillows, work boots for the walks in the forest, and
a folding chair he had redone the wood, and
put in the new cloth in the seating area. He had
his bathroom items; towels; his Bible; his little book; a twenty-five-foot electric cord; tape
player for music (only the Moody Blues); and
this time money to pay for gas, the campsite,

and ice. When he leaves, he tells no one. He just blasts off to Jupiter. As he is driving through the small town of Jupiter, he remembers the walk he had on the road in the hot sun in his sandals and his feet sore.

The weather is a lot cooler here. It is December 1, and it's only seven in the morning. He's the first one to sign up for the campsite, but they open at eight, so he sits in the VW and reads the Word.

"Now the God of hope fill you with all joy and peace in believing, that you may abound in hope, through the power of the Holy Spirit" (Romans 15:13). "But the Lord is the true God, he is the living God, and an everlasting King: at his wrath the earth shall tremble" (Jeremiah 10:10).

When they open, he tells the park ranger he would like to pay for forty-five days. He is so sure he will make the forty days of fasting. No one knows what the next day may bring. The ranger tells him only two weeks at a time. The ranger shows him on the map of how big Jonathan Dickerson Park is. He asks if he could drive to the sites and pick one out and come back with the lot number. The ranger tells him, "Sure!" He drives his red VW bug down a long straight road with trees all around. You can't see the forest fore the trees.

"Strive to enter in at the strait gate: for many, I say unto you, will seek to enter in, and shall not be able" (Jesus).

It takes about ten minutes to get to one of the areas where people camp. The campsites down by the river he did not want to go to. He sees one camper here now, as he is driving around the 235 campsites, in between the trees; when Christmas gets here, it will be filled. He picks out a good lot not too far from the bathrooms but not too close either to hear the noise. The lot must be big enough not to hear the noise of neighbors, and if any friends drives up from Fort Lauderdale and need car space for parking and a place to put up another tent, there will be space available. He drives back to the ranger's post. No one is here yet, and he signs up for two weeks. The ranger tells him he can sign up every two weeks for three months in the same spot but must sign up the day before due date. "Yes, sir! I understand." He picks out some information on the park. "Thank you, sir," as he walks out the door.

Back at the campsite, he gets his electric cord out and hooks up to the AC outlet that each campsite has. Let's get the music going putting the Moody Blues in the air. As he gets everything out of the car, he puts things on the picnic table. He puts his chair in front of where the fire will be tonight. Where he will be setting up the tent, he gathers pine needles to soften the bottom of the tent. Those needles will not go through that strong army tent bottom. Then he sets up the tent. It's big enough for six people to sleep in. He then puts a big blanket on the floor inside of the tent to make it even softer where he will sleep. There will be no shoes worn on the inside either; he puts the sleeping bag in the back corner, then his clothes, the fruits, and nuts so the animals will not get into it.

As he takes a step back out and looks in at the master bedroom; all is well. He leaves out the ice chest with a pint of milk, water, orange juice, and ice tea, which is homemade with lemons. He sits in his chair of his master's living room, the great outdoors, and listens to the Moody's fifth album, *Question of Balance*; as he takes a walk around the campsite to get his firewood for the next day or two, because no one here the tree branches were all over in the area where his campsite is and it's very peaceful with the Moody Blues in the air it takes about an hour, till the tape is done. He sits in his chair and thanks the Lord for everything. He reads in his Bible, and he opens it up to John 14: "Let not your heart be trouble; you believe in God, believe also in me. I am the way, the truth, and the life: no man comes unto the Father but by me. Believe me that I am in the Father, and the Father in me: or else believe me for the very works sake. Verily, verily, I say unto you, he that believes on me, the works that I do shall he do also; and greater works than these shall he do; because I go unto the Father." Reading to the end of John, he picks up the little book and reads from cover to cover. He feels the love in his heart and mind.

The fire has dimmed to ashes, and he gets up from his chair and walks to the tent, unzips the tent flap, takes off his shoes, gets in, picks up his sandals, brushes off the bottoms with a shoe brush, and puts them in the front corner of the tent. He would like to keep the inside of his tent dirt-free. Then to test the bed with the pine needles, it's extra soft cushion for a good night sleep. As he lies on his sleeping bag, it's quite outside, and he said a prayer. This is the end of the first day, and thirty-nine days to go, and at the end, he prays he will be a more enlightened human being and be more like Christ—healing the sick, help the blind see, walk on water, turn water into wine, and raise the dead all through Jesus's name.

He rises early before the dawn. He prays as he does every morning, noon, and night. Any time is good to talk to your heavenly Father. He is always there and never leaves or forsakes you. You just need to believe.

He is in and out of the restroom before the very few other campers think of getting up. Plus, he loves seeing the sunrise. It takes him back to his younger days. He goes to a place where there is an opening, thru the trees so to see the beauty unfold. The thrill is not as beautiful as when you're on the beaches, but each time is different no matter where you are on earth. This he will do for three days a week while he is here. Then off he goes for his walk and gathers wood. The more wood, the better, and he picks up little plants for the terrariums, he will be making to kill the time while on the fast. He wants a more perfect way of being more like Christ. It's been said it takes thirty days to start a new habit. You know, we only have 24,640 days here on earth, that's if we get to live to seventy years old. It's not a lot if that's all we got, but we have eternity; now that's long.

There were not very many campers, but as time gets closer to Christmas, every campsite will be taken, and the noise at times will be all around. He can hear the quiet in the air. Do you ever go to the closet, the quiet place, to talk to your heavenly Father? "Therefore, prophesy thou against them all these words, and say unto them, the Lord shall roar from on high, and utter his voice from his Holy habitation; he shall mightily roar upon his habitation; he shall give a shout, as they that tread the grapes, against all the inhabitance of the earth" (Jeremiah 25:30).

"Then shall you call upon me, and you shall go and pray unto me, and I will hearken unto you. And you shall seek me, and find me, when you shall search for me with all your heart" (Jeremiah 29:12–13).

He can smell the bacon in the air, so he drinks a glass of orange juice and chews on the nuts to make the hunger pains go away. He'll have a glass of milk for lunch and dinner with a few soybeans and the fruit, orange, banana, and apple as the fast starts. After those three days, he is out of these items, and he only has water and soybeans for the next three days. After that, on the seventh day, he'll only drinks water from that day on. The next three days are the toughest. That pain keeps hitting you in the stomach, saying, "Where's the food, you fool?" Days go by slowly, but it's sweet as pie to focus on God, in nature, plus having no pot or beer to mess up your mind by thinking of sex, drugs, or rock and roll. The days go by slow, and the nights go by fast, and in a blink of an eye, five days have passed. It's Friday. He is just reading, "Look unto me, and be you saved, all the ends of the earth: for I am God, and there is none else" (Isaiah 45:22). It's about one hour before sunset, and he hears some swearing through the woods north west of his campsite. He gets up and walks through the trees that separate him from them. He introduces himself to the young couple and asks if he could help. The young man tells him he is having trouble with the tent, that he can use a little help. They work together, and the tent is up and ready as the darkness is coming over then. They talk for a while about life, and the couple tells Freddy they are getting married next weekend and they would like him to come. He tells them he loves to and says good night. He sees them again before they check out on Sunday afternoon. Back at his campsite, he throws more wood to his fire for the night. He thinks of the time Jesus went to the wedding feast when he turned water into wine as the flames burn higher and higher. The song from the third album of the Moody Blues goes through the air.

Blasting, billowing, bursting forth with the power of ten billion butterflies sneezes, man with his flaming fire has conquered the wayward breezes, climbing to tranquility far above the cloud conceiving the heavens clear of misty shroud. Higher and higher now we've learned to play with fire go higher and higher vast vision must improve our sight perhaps at last, we'll see an end to our endless blight. And the beginning of the free, clime to tranquility finding it's real worth, conceiving the heavens flourishing on earth. Higher and higher now we've learned to play with fire go higher and higher.

Another song from the same album:

> Something you can't hide, says your lonely, hidden deep inside of you only, it's there for you to see, take a look and be. Burn slowly the candle of life. Something there outside, says we're only, in the hands of time, falling slowly, it's there for us to know, with love that we can go, burn slowly the candle of life. So, love everybody and make them your friend.

Jesus said that, right? "A new commandment I give unto you: Love one another, As I have loved you, so you must love one another" (John 13:34). You see how the Moodys are a spiritual musical group, and he knows it's true.

He shakes his head to get out of the dream of the music he loves so much, sitting in front of the fire. He gets up and walks out to the dirt road. He turns and looks in at his living quarters with the fire going, then looks up to the stars. He knows how real God is. After ten minutes, in a flash, one star shoots by. He thanks the Creator and walks back to sits in the chair and reads the Word.

Paul, an apostle of Jesus Christ by the will of God, said to the saints who were at Ephesus and to the faithful in Christ Jesus:

"Grace be to you, and peace, from God our Father, and from the Lord Jesus Christ. Blessed be the God and Father of our Lord Jesus Christ, who has blessed us with all spiritual blessing in heavenly places in Christ. According as he has chosen us in him before the foundation of the world, that we should be holy and without blame before him in love: Having predestinated us unto the adoption of children by Jesus Christ himself, according to the good pleasure of his will, To the praise of the glory of his grace, wherein he has made us accepted in the beloved. In whom we have redemption through his blood, the forgiveness of sin, according to the riches of his grace; wherein he has abounded toward us in all wisdom and prudence; Having made known unto us the mystery of his will, according to his good pleasure which he has purposed in himself."

He puts down his Bible. This is Christ within us. The knowledge and wisdom of God is so great. The whole human race can be one with God in his Christ. It's God's Christ that's within us, but we call it the Holy Spirit. The Father would like us to be like his Christ, God letting himself be a man, walking on this earth and calling himself Yasha, Jesus! The Holy Spirit is enlightening young Freddy to how great it is being loved by him. That love he experiences after his walk to Daytona Beach, he wants more and to know his calling. What is this timing between the music and the Word? He goes for another walk. He likes to talk to the Father on his walks. He'd asks, "What is my mission here on earth?" He passes young lovers on his way to be just him and the Lord—no noise. After a couple pass him by, he sings a song from the first album of the Moody Blues, and he sings it out loud.

Nights white Stain never reaching the end, letters I've written never meaning to send. Beauty I've always missed, with these eyes before. Just what the truth is, I can't say any more. Cause I love you, yes, I love you. Ho how I love you. Gazing at people, some hand in hand, just what I'm going through they can't understand. Some try to tell me thoughts they can not defend, just what you want to be, you'll be in the end. And I love you, oh yes! I love you, O how, I love you.

He sings that over and over for about seven minutes into the walk. He is telling the Father, Son, and Holy Spirit he loves the three of them as one.

Then the song "Questions," from the fifth album, *Questions of Balance*, pops into his mind.

Why do we never get an answer when we're knocking at the door, with a thousand million questions about hate and death and war. It's when we stop and look around us there is nothing that we need! In a world of persecution that is burning in it's greed. Why do we never get an answer when we're knocking at the door? Because the truth is hard to swallow, that's what the war of love is for. It's not the way that you say it when you do those things to me. It's more the way that you mean it when you tell me what will be. And when you stop, and think about it, you won't believe it's true. That all the love you've been giving, has all been meant for you. I'm looking for someone to change my life. I'm looking for a miracle in my life. And if you could see what it's done to me. To lose the love I knew that could safely lead me through, between the silence of the mountains and the crashing of the sea. There lies a land I once lived in and she is waiting there for me. But in the grey of the morning my mind becomes confused between the dead and the sleeping and the road that I must choose. I'm looking for someone to change my life, I'm looking for a miracle in my life.

He has memorized the songs from all six albums, just like he has learned all the thoughts in the little book by heart. In each album, there's one idea that recurs over and over: love. He reads the Bible, "God is love" (1 John).

"If one should desire to know whether a Kingdom is well governed, if its morals are good or bad, the quality of its music, will furnish the answer" (Confucius).

The first album with Justin Hayward and John Lodge is *Days of Future Past*. The rest of the band members, Ray Thomas, Mike Pinter, Gram Edge were the ones who formed the Moody Blues; but when Justin and John joined the band, they brought in the completeness of wisdom, and all the members became more spiritual minded, using a different sound and words of wisdom, which made them complete. This first album was way ahead of its time, and only few had ears to hear. The London Philharmonic Orchestra played on the album, and Justin's number one song was "Nights in White Satin," which was played a lot on the radio. This song, to Freddy, is saying, "You are part of God! You have sent letters to him by prayers to know him. Yes! Get closer to the Father of the universe." Then the song in the same album "Tuesday

Afternoon" was very popular. The way the whole album was, "You are one with everything. Oh! How I love thee. Jesus's love is the best love ever. He died for You and Me."

Then the second album is *In Search of the Lost Cord*. The first song was "Departure." This is the song that gave Freddy the light in his mind to search for Christ. This album is the sound of the far east. It will send you into meditation. Do you remember Timothy Leary? On the cover of the album, the picture you can look at is about birth and death. The message is between birth and death. There is spiritual awakening. What are you doing spiritually thinking?

The third album was *To Our Children Children's Children*.

What a moving and enlightened bunch of songs. It starts off with "Higher and Higher," a song you must listen to through headphones. If truth be told, all the Moody Blues albums should be listened to through headphones. There are musical sounds that you cannot hear without headphones, the sounds that blow you away; but the words were truth, love God, family, and friends. The fourth album is *On a Threshold of a Dream*.

This album is the one he heard at the party in the summer of 1969, just before Freddy got married. Some of his friends started smoking pot, but Freddy was so against smoking he stayed away from them at the party when they smoked. The song was the "Dream" that catches his attention. It was like all the noise stopped at the party, but this song. From that point of time, the music was calling him, and he was in love with the Moody Blues's music. After buying the three albums, it was like they were speaking to him personally. He was totally into the music and what they had to say. It was all meant to be, burn slowly the candle of life.

The fifth was *Question of Balance*.

This album was so filled with wisdom of the Father, Son, and Spirit. The Moodys are guiding you to a deeper and clearer understanding of life in love. We should live on earth with love in our hearts. Take the minister's song. It's all about Christ's love. Take time to hear it again.

The sixth was *Every Good Boy Deserves Favor*.

When you take the first letter from each word *E, G, B, D, F*. These are the notes that are on each bar of the sheet music that you would read if playing a musical instrument. This was genius for the music world back in 1971. The album cover with and old man holding in his hand gems and a little boy with eyes wide open with his finger pointing at the sprinkling gems, wanting to touch the light. The music and words were leading Freddy on a spiritual quest; all the words were on each album meet even more to him. It was as if each one was leading him to find a better way of getting closer to God within and without, just like the bubble of love he had after being baptizes the love was in and all around him. Then he read it in the Bible where Jesus said, "The kingdom of God is within you." He's beginning to hear and see there is more, an even deeper purpose behind the words and the music of the Moody Blues.

"Pass the minor on the wall who's the biggest fool of all? Don't you feel small, it happens to us all" (Moody Blues).

Freddy's dyslexia all through his youth, keep him from reading, but with the albums of the Moodys, he would hear the words in the music, and because the record came in a sleeve and they had the words to each song printed on that sleeve of paper, well, that help him read and memorize the words to each song. He followed along day after day from 1969 until now, coming to the end of 1973 being on his fast.

Each day has gone by pretty much the same, and he is on the fourteenth day of his fasting. The park is getting close to being full of folks, families, with lots of young kids playing. On that day in the park on his walk, two boys ask him to play catch football. He still loves the game, so he goes out for a pass not too far. He runs around with them for about three to seven minutes, and he starts feeling very lightheaded, sick in the stomach. Not eating just hit him big-time. He sits on a picnic table, and he tells the boys he had enough. He walks back to camp very dizzy, weak, feeling sick. He drinks some water and takes a nap. He sleeps all that day and through the night.

The next day, he is still weak, and he sits and drinks water and eats a handful of soybeans he was feeding the squeals with, trying to get some energy. It helps, and he puts on the music and reads the words to each song, and he understands more on each album. Each album leads you to the next and has the same meaning, and all albums lead you to one thought: *love* God *and each other*. How easy does that sound, yet we people of earth take the wrong road of hate, hate this, hate that. When we put on Christ, that is let the Holy Spirit work in you, then we will have peace, yes! Helping, and loving one another. "Your kingdom come, your will be done" (Matthew 6:10).

After hours of the Moody Blues, he is moved by the Holy Spirit, put Christ in every thought in the little book, and to look in the Bible, and put the scripture with thoughts. He reads the little book and starts putting Christ Jesus as the main theme in each thought in the little book. To love like Christ loved us, that's what we really need to do. "Happiest is determined by the number of persons one loves." He adds the words "with a heart of Christ" (1 Peter 3:14–22 and 2:21).

To love like the Master loves, Freddy has felt that love there is no greater love than that, but can you love like Christ? Can you give up all for Christ?

"If you are suffering from a bad man's injustice, forgive him lest there be two bad men" (Romans 12:17–21).

Teachings from the Master. Men arrange words to sound like they know what, but it all comes from the Father, not us; it's God working in us, some people have not figured it out yet. We need to take the time to hear the voice of the Holy Spirit.

"The language that God hears best is the silent language of love." He adds, "Christ's love" (Matthew 6:14).

"Whoever has a heart full of love always has something to give." He adds, "Christ's love" (John 3:16–21).

"We are shaped and fashioned by what we love." He adds focus on "Christ's love" (Proverbs 23:7, Luke 6:45, Luke 12:15, 24).

"Never treat the worst those whom you love the best" (Titus). Read all and Luke 6:27, 35–35, Luke 12:37).

Jesus the Christ of God said, "Love your enemies." That's not easy for us selfish humans. It's God in us that helps us to love others and our enemies.

People may doubt what you say, but they always believe what you do. In your Bible, read John 14:10–15.

This will take time, for there are over a hundred thoughts in the little book, so each time he reads his Bible, he looks for the connection with the thought and with scripture.

The Holy Spirit helps in his thinking, the love for the Lord Jesus, that leads to joy in your soul, and a purpose in your life to love everyone, and make them your friend. Let this pour out into every area of your life and bring new and better spiritual love to all you are guided to meet. His mind is renewed, and he goes for a walk to pick up wood for the fire. The weather is changing. It's getting colder at night, and a good fire is a pleasure to have, the light, warmth, and the dancing flames.

It's Monday, time to register for another two weeks, so he drives to the office. As he is walking up to the office door, three young men are coming out, and one is saying to the other, "Where are we going to stay? Every place we have gone is booked." Freddy goes in and asks the park ranger because it is full he is not sure if he is allowed to have two cars on his space and more people to stay for a couple of days. The ranger tells him he is allowed to have up to three cars and twelve people on his campsite. He tells the ranger he'll be right back. He catches up to the boys before they get to their van. He tells them that they can stay on his campsite till they can find another site and they have two weeks. All you must do is pay the seventeen dollars parking fee. They hand Freddy the money, and he goes in to sign up for the two weeks, for all to stay if they need to. When he comes out of the office, he tells them follow him to the campsite. They drive down the straight road to the entrance to all the campsites filled with campers. He parks in his spot gets out of the car, and shows them where to park. The three boys get out of the van with boundless joy for the deed that has happen to them. Then the van door opens and one pretty girl gets out, then another, another, and another all very pretty. Each one gives Freddy a big hug, four girls and three guys. What are the odds of that? Freddy's thinking it is another test from the Father. He is tempted, and he must be strong to go through this one. He tells the boys and girls where the restrooms are and tells them all to get some wood for their fire. The girls leave, and the boys tell Freddy their names. "I'm Doc, going to school to be a doctor." They shake hands. "I'm James, going for the fun of it." "I'm Danny, business law for right now." Freddy helps the guys set up their tents. The kids our all from a college in upstate New York. Freddy leaves, telling them all, "If you need any help, you know where I live." After a good hour, the girls come back with lots of wood for the cool night. The kids get things in order and leave for the boat rentals, which is about a twenty-minute ride away. This park is big. At home, Freddy cleans up his area and does his daily reading in the Bible, Proverbs 5:1 to end.

"My son, attend unto my wisdom, and bow thine ear to my understanding: that thou mayest regard discretion, and that thy lips may keep knowledge. For the lips of a strange woman drop as a honeycomb, and her mouth is smoother than oil: But her end is bitter as wormwood, sharp as a two-edged sword. Her feet go down to death; her steps take hold on hell." After reading, he does some mediation, then his daily walk.

By five o'clock, the kids are back. It gets dark by six, and off they go to the restrooms. As they walk past Freddy, they ask if he would like some dinner with them. He tells them, "Thanks! No, thank you." He does not want them to know of his fasting.

Their dinner is over, and one of the girls walks over to Freddy's camp. "Hi! My name is Delia. We are done eating, and can you come over now?" He puts down the little book he was reading, puts it in his Bible, and puts them in the tent. They walk over to the kids' camp, and everyone introduces themselves again. Then Doc stands up and speaks. "Freddy, we are so grateful for what you have done. As a group, we say…" And they all say "Thank you," in unison.

As he is sitting at the picnic table, he asks if anyone has heard of the Moody Blues. They say, "Yes, we have heard of the name. We might know some of their songs. Well, let me tell you one." He stands up. "Breath deep the cantering gloom, watch lights fade from every room. Bunches of people look back and lament, another day useless, and year sent. Passionate lovers wrestle as one, lonely man cries for love, and have none; new Mother picks up and suckles her son. Senior citizens wish they were young. Cold hearted orb that rules the night remover the colors from our site. Red is gray, and yellow white, but we dissuade what is right and what is and elision."

Looking at them, he can tell they are not expecting that. He tells them, "You've got to hear the music as well. Each album has one whole meaning. And that meaning is love! Now let me tell you a thought out of the little book. 'Love does not consist in gazing at each other, but in looking forward together in the same direction.' I'm looking forward for more of Christ's love. 'Only in loving Christ can life's true path be made way. Christ love is self-giving; therefore, love is God.' We learn to understand God by the reading of his word out of his Holy Bible. Which Jesus has taught us, 'If a man loves me, he will keep my words: and my Father will love him, and we will come unto him, and make our abode with him.' 'This is my commandment, that you love one another, as I have loved you.'

"One more thought out of the little book. 'Each act we perform from motives of Christ love pours strength and health into the stream of life. Hate causes us to perish, sometimes in a series of little deaths, sometimes at once. If we would preserve life in its fullest sense, we must choose the course of Christ's love' (Smiley Blanton). That's the sermon for tonight. That's all I'll say on Christ's love."

The guys hand Freddy a beer, and he does not refuse it. He will just sip on it as the night goes on. He knows the protein in it will be good for him on his forty-day fast. The girls ask for more poetry. He tells them, "Later, let me hear about you all." Each one tells their story as the evening goes on. By eleven, he ends up in the van playing cards with all four girls. They have been drinking beer most of the night and are in happy spirits. A good hour has passed, and Freddy tells the girls it's time to turn in. They all get out of the van, and one of the girls whispers in his ear, asking if she can sleep with him. He believes Delia does not want to sleep in the van with all the girls so he said ok, but he tells her, "You know I'm on a spiritual sojourn, so no kissing no touching." With a little smile on that cute face, Delia says, "Okay!" They all say good night, and the two walk over to his campsite. The fire is burning only coals, so there is no light to see. He picks up and turns on his flashlight that is on his picket table and walks over to the tent. He unzips it, and he takes off his sandals, gets in the tent, brushes off the dirt, and puts them on the floor by the entranceway. He then moves some things around. Then he tells her to remove her shoes before coming in, brush the dirt off, then pull the zipper down. She lies down. Then he lies next to her on the sleeping area. He gives Delia a pillow. Then they lay the sheets over them and a blanket, then the heavy sleeping bag open to cover them both. The air is very cold. It goes down to their bones. Freddy knows two are better than one in the chilly night for warmth. They lie side by side to keep warm, and he turns off the light. Five minutes goes by, and Delia turns to Freddy and starts to kiss him, showing him she is a little hungry for love. His first reaction is to kiss her back. She is very pretty. Then he stops. He tells her, "I cannot do this, I'm sorry." He turns around with his back to Delia, thinking of the scripture he read earlier in the morning, and he goes into a deep sleep. Sometime in the night, Delia gets up and walks back to the van to sleep, disturbing the other girls.

When Freddy gets up in the early morning, she is gone, and he is thinking only good thoughts about how noble he was for not kissing with Delia, but when he says hello to the kids, he is surprised by their unfriendliness, and

Freddy's not sure why it is, maybe because he did not even make out or have any sexual desires for Delia. Then Doc tells Freddy they are moving and they will not bother him anymore. Before this, he is on a spiritual high from his fasting for twenty-one days.

This crushes his earthly heart very much, and he goes from feeling good spiritually to a piece of crap. He is very sorry to have made the new friends uncomfortable because he had no sexual advance on Delia. They are out to party, not to get close to God. He thinks he would have a nice fellowshipping with them for a few more days. It's not that long ago he was drinking like a fool at the parties. Freddy walks back to his camp dazed and confused. He sits in his chair and thinks about sex. *Maybe you do not have to be married to have a physical relationship*, he thinks. He is alone with himself and his heavenly Father, his best friend. It's Tuesday afternoon, and they are gone. He opens his Bible and reads, "That Christ may dwells in your hearts by faith; that you, being rooted and grounded in love (Christ's love)" (Ephesians 3:17).

"Who so ever therefore shall break one of these least commandments, and shall teach men so, he shall be called the least in the kingdom of heaven: but who so ever shall do, and teach them, the same shall be called great in the kingdom of heaven" (Matthew 5:19).

He reads in the little book, "The best portion of a good man's life is his little nameless, unremembered acts of kindness and of love" (William Wordsworth). "The great tragedy of life is not that people perish, but that they cease to love Christ and his teachings."

What are our two needs? Someone to love us, the Father, someone for us to love, Jesus, God's Christ.

The Holy Spirit fills his heart with love. He stops reading, and he's not a lonely man looking for love. He has the highest love within, the Holy Spirit of the Father of the universe. He gets up to start his campfire, then goes for a walk. His heart and mind are filled with Christ's love. He's a happy camper, as night comes, and in the evening, he is sitting in his chair by the fire, in the cool of the night, and then a young boy walks up to the fire light. Freddy sees he is just a little disoriented. They talk for a minute, and then Freddy asks if he knows Jesus. The boy answers yes! Freddy asks, "Is he in your heart?" He answers yes! "That's good. He's in mine too." The boy smiles. He feels safe, and he sits at the picnic table. They talk for seven minutes, and then the boy gets up and leaves. It is like he just flowed into camp and reinsured Freddy's faith in Christ, then flowed out of camp. Five days have gone by, and Doc stops over. He invites Freddy over for dinner and drinks, and says, "You can say goodbye to the others. We're leaving to go back to school."

He shows him on a map where their campsite location is, down by the river. Freddy said, "Yea, that sounds nice." Doc said, "We would not be here if you did not help us. We are all thankful. You will stop by?" "Not much said, but, yes, I'll stop by." Doc drives off. He thinks about the young girl who hated him for not sleeping with her. The thought in the little book tells him, "Each act we perform from motives of 'Christ' love, pours strength and health into the stream of life. Hate causes us to perish, sometimes in a series of little deaths, sometimes at once. If we would preserve life in its fullest sense, we must choose the course of Christ love" (Smiley Blanton).

The Bible tells us the same. "For this is the message that you have heard from the beginning, that we should love one another. We know that we have passed from death unto life, because we love the brethren. He that loveth not his brother abideth in death. Whosoever hated his brother is a murderer: And this is his commandment, that we should believe on the name of his son Jesus the Christ and love one another, as he gave us commandment. And he that keeps his commandment dell in him, and he in him, and here by we know that he abideth in us, by the Spirit which he has given us" (1 John 3:11, 14, 15 and 3:23, 24). Hallelujah!

That night, he ends his twenty-seventh day of fasting. The kids do not know he is fasting just God. He pulls up in his VW bug. He has brought a big fish to be put on the grill. He hugs them all. Freddy has prepared a prayer at dinner to say. "There is one body and one Spirit even as you are called in one hope of your calling. One Lord, one faith, one baptism, one God, and Father of all, who is above all, and through all, and in you all. But unto every one of us is given *grace* according to the measure of the gift of Christ. Hallelujah! Father, thank you for your grace, amen."

"The law gives us the knowledge of sin." They all have some food, drinks, and laughter way late into the night. Then they hug and say their goodbyes. He almost forgot, Delia has met a man whom she found at this campsite.

The drive back to the campsite is very slow. The drinking is little but effective. The next day, Freddy wakes up late, with a bad headache from the booze. The old saying is true, "With booze, you lose! But with dope, there is hope for your sorry ass!" He thinks he has blown his oneness with the Father; he's gone from spiritual thinking back to earthly stinking thinking. That is why Jesus came and died for the sins of the entire world—the good news, for all your sins. The Father never stops loving you. Do you know Jesus? If you know him, then you know you are forgiven for your decision you have made. Forgive yourself and try again. The Spirit of Christ dwells within you.

Freddy is disappointed with himself. His heart is burning for the love of the Father. He believes he failed his heavenly Father. Your earthly desires will stay with you until Christ comes back. He must control them, and it's not as easy as 1, 2, 3. Freddy does not know that you must let the Holy Spirit do it.

The morning is cool. He goes back to sleep, to sleep off the hangover. He becomes a fool. With booze, you lose, but with dope, there's hope for your sorry ass!

He couldn't stand the pain, knowing he tried to be like Christ in vain, just to be one with his love; now the curtain has fallen. He was weak. He partied with the earthly desires. Where does he go from here? He falls into a deep sleep all through the night, and he wakes in the morning; the booze has worn off. He has two more days. Then his permit is ended. He reads his Bible. "Look unto me, and be you saved, all the ends of the earth: for I am God, and there is none else" (Isaiah 45:22). There is so much spiritual food in the sixty-six books of the Bible, and he still has the love for it all, plus his little book, and the Moody Blues. The days go by slow. He's not making his forty-day fast to be one with the Father, Son, and Holy Spirit. Nothing more to do but pack up his tent and puts things in the VW. He drives back to Fort Lauderdale very disappointed. The only good thing he knows once you have Christ, he never leaves you. Plus, he knows more about the music and his mission.

# Chapter 5

## Question of Balance

"Why do we never get an answer when we are knocking at the door, with a thousand million questions about hate, death, and war. When we stop, and look around us there is nothing that we need, in a world of precaution that is burning in it greed."

Two hours later, and he has gotten a room at a hotel, and he calls his ex-wife to make plans. He is going to stop by to see his little girls and to take them for the weekend. On the same day, he calls the ex-boss and gets his job back.

The seventh album of the Moody Blues has come out while he was on his fast, so now he buys it, and after he hears the whole album, a light goes off in his mind. It's the words in the song "You and Me." He knows by the Holy Spirit that the Moody Blues have done it. Each past album has brought you to an awaking that God is love, and the seventh album is the apex. The seventh album brings you to Christ and the Father love, with the song "You and Me." Hear the words to the song: "There is a leafless tree in Asia, under the sun theirs a holist man, there's a forest fire in the valley where the story all began. What will be are last thought do you think it's coming soon? Will it be of comfort, or the pain of a burning wound? All we are trying to say is we are all we've got. You and Me just cannot fail if we never ever stop. You're an ocean filled with faces, and you know that we believe we're just a wave that drifts around you, singing all our hopes and dreams. We look around and wonder at the work that has been done by the visions of our Father's touch by his lovely Son. All we are trying to say is we are all we got. You and me cannot fail if we never ever stop."

By the Holy Spirit, it's been revealed to Freddy that the Moody Blues from the *Days of*

*Future Past* album to the *Seventh Sojourn* album bring you to Christ, of the Father and his love. His fasting in the campgrounds helped him to focus on the words and the music, and to wait to hear from God, and all along coming back from his sojourn the Father reveals his Christ in the seventh album. How cool is that? Seven times seven is forty-nine.

The next day, he calls the Moody Blues headquarters in England; their operation is so big now, and he would like to talk to Justin Hayward but only gets their fan operator. He tries to let them know how special the seven albums are and how each album's message led him to the next album's message, and the seventh album, called the *Seventh Sojourn*, brings you to Christ Jesus. He is blown off as a nut. The Holy Spirit has opened his mind to this truth of which God has put together from the beginning of time. What are the odds of that to happen? Only once in a lifetime. He tries for a month to get in touch, but they just hang up on him. The Father's timing is everything! Freddy decides to put this truth on the back burner, but it's God's plan when he wants it to come out. Freddy just keeps all this in his heart and mind; he's only a messenger.

Months have gone by. Now he's renting an old house off Dixie highway. Coming home from a hard backbreaking workday, he falls onto the bed facedown. He asks the Father in thought to heal his aching back. Just as he finishes asking, he feels a hand touch him right where it hurt on his back. It is so real, and it scares him, and he jumps out of bed looking all around to see if any real person is there. The touch was so real. Now he knows for sure God still loves him. He knows he was just touched by our loving Father, and he thanks him with a happy heart. How beautiful that touch was. His pain is gone, looking at the bed, knowing God the Father how real. He just touches him, and he felt the hand of God touch him. Hallelujah! The Father never leaves you or forsakes you. The Holy Spirit of God puts himself in you, and he is there living in you. His love is so wonderful, and all you must do is have faith and believe in a man called Yasha, Jesus the Christ of God, our heavenly Father, as a man on earth, who shed his blood for your sins, died and has risen again, letting us know there is life after death on eternity's road. So just believe in Jesus the Christ of the Father. Try to live as he lived, loving all his creation, all his children. You see, he came down and planted a part of himself in a woman to be among his chosen people—the Israelites. "Surely, shall one say, in the Lord have I righteousness and strength: even to him shall men come: and all that are incensed against him shall be ashamed. In the Lord shall all the seed of Israel be justified, and shall glory" (Isaiah 45:24–25).

You see, if you believe in Yasha, you are Israel, which means a prince of God. Because of his grace, he shows us how much he loves us. Because he shed his blood, we get to stand in his presence. We who believe, we have eternal life. Death, where is your sting? He makes it known in your mind and heart he is real.

"I can do all things through Christ which strengthened me" (Philippians 4:13). You will never understand all of God; but to know he is within you, how can you not enjoy life, love one another, help each other see the truth, live the truth? You are Israel, a prince of God, a child of the most high, how precious is that?

He is going to a small church. They preach the word, and the word is love. "Say the word and you will be free, say the word and be like me, say the word I'm thinking of, have you heard the word is Love" (John Lennon).

Freddy is involved with believers. Next to knowing is knowing where to find out, and that's asking your heavenly Father. He has and is experiencing the spiritual side of the Father's love. Studying his Bible every day, he has read thru the Holy Bible from cover to cover seven times. He knows he has a personal relationship with the Father, Son, Holy Spirit, and the love, and he is here for a calling out that's coming in the Father's timing. Freddy starts to put his life down on paper.

After work on Friday, all the men would go to the bar and drink and smoke pot. He would pick up his two daughters, and Dad always plans on a fun time for the weekend. He brings them home Sunday night to their mother and stepdad.

Weeks, months, and a year go by. He's not dating anyone, but he still hangs out with church friends and the group of friends he grew up with. He has one foot on the sea of Christ's love and one foot on the earthly things like money, love, hate, death, and war. The human side of us always likes the earthly, but he has tasted the spiritual side of God's love. He knows how real Jesus is, and he thanks Jesus always in all he does.

One Tuesday afternoon, Freddy and a friend stop at the Dairy Queen to get a thick chocolate shake and an orange blizzard, which is a habit for them whenever they get together, and they have been on this habit for months. Freddy gets out of the VW bug. He walks up to the window and looks right into the blue eyes of a pretty young girl, the owner's daughter. It was his first time ever seeing her, and he feels a great love coming over him just by looking in her eyes. The stare was like the one he felt in Daytona Beach, locking eyes with Sarah, but this one was with lightning running thru his veins straight to his heart. It is real earthy love for this girl. There was no sexual desire to look in her eyes, and it is pure love running through his heart and mind.

The love is not as big and bold as the Father's love, but it was the timing, being alone, and not searching, but being found to love and be loved. They talk for a while, for she is filled with the same spirit of love. He got her name and phone number, and takes the shakes, and gets back in the car and took off knowing he is in love the highest level for a girl he has ever felt, to this date.

She comes out of his dreams into his heart. She is only sixteen, and she is his Diary Queen. Oh, how he loves her. She is his Eve on earth but a heavenly delight. Throughout the day, he thinks about what time to call her in the evening. The love is a drug he could not get enough of. Just looking into her eyes is purely lovely. They start dating, and she is very smart, and at seventeen, she graduates from high school. The love between them is going for a year and half, and she knows about the children and his love for the

Lord. Her actions show she has a love for them but not for the Lord. They decide to get married. He plans the music with his good friends he knows who play guitars. Then together, they find a cute chapel, and three months later, they get married. The wedding is beautiful; everything is perfect.

Two months into the marriage, the new wife admits she just pretended to like his daughters when they were dating. His very precious girls, she tells him they should stay out of their lives. "It's just you and me with no kids, no church, or I will leave you." Funny how the song from the seventh album of the Moody's "You and Me" says how we should love one another, and she hates the Lord and his little girls.

He is blown away. He can't believe what his ears are hearing. How can he stop loving the Lord? How can he cut his daughters out of his life, see them no more, remove them from his heart? That can't be, but his love for this girl is so real. It's not possible; this cannot be true. He tells her he will not be part of that picture, she leaves him that day, and in one month, he receives the annulment papers. It's over—that quick. Love comes in, and your heart is rip out. The Father's love will always be with you, but Freddy is heartbroken. His earthly love is gone.

Heartbroken, he is not thinking right; he's dazed and confused; love hurts, but what did Christ do for us, his sacrifice, and his pain? It's the light living in God's Holy thoughts, he has for you and me. Freddy starts to smoke pot more often. It's not just for reading anymore. God is still in his heart, but the world and all the temptations are darkening his mind. He is going to take a walk on the other side of life. He is walking out of the light into the darkness. "But still his hand is stretched out" (Isaiah 14:24-32 & 45:7).

"Another morning, another day upon the sea, following the breezes, it's like a dream come true. There's no storm warning; it's just steady as she goes, the wind tickling my nose, till the day is through. "Oh! Great! Another beautiful sunset. It's just like I always dreamed. Living life in paradise is harder than it seems. Fishing is thrilling but I hate cleaning out the bones, drinking all alone, talking to myself. Shimmy me timbres the stars are big and bright, a real romantic night with no one else. The breathtaking sunrise, it's like an angel watching over me. It's being haunted by everything that you dreamed"" (Unknown).

He drifted from the Father's love to the dark side. "Woe to those who call evil good and good evil, who put darkness for light and light for darkness" (Isaiah 5:20).

Construction work died in South Florida, so he has to work two jobs to make the same amount of money as he did in construction. After seven months, one of the jobs finally gives him enough hourly money, so he leaves the other job, and work for one. Now he is full-time putting together a battery booster machine; they are renting them to car dealers, and two weeks out of the month, he's driving around to service the machines at different car dealerships, locations from Homestead to Jupiter in south Florida. He is meeting lots of people and making new friends. He knew the owner, mechanics, and down to the young men who wash the cars at each place he services. Freddy starts off with buying a pound of pot, then breaking it down into sixteen-ounce bags, then placing each one in a big brown bag like the ones you get in the grocery story before plastic bags came out, and he gives the guys who smoke pot the best deal if they buy from him. He sells them weight ounces, a free pack of rolling papers, at a fair price. Every time he makes a friend, he talks about Jesus, his love, grace, and mercy through the Holy Spirit is within him; so he is reaching people who might not have even heard of Jesus. When the Holy Spirit is in you, he never leaves you. You cannot stop talking about Christ. Is not happy better than sad? So finding happiness in Christ Jesus is always the solution.

Freddy's thinking pot fixed his dyslexia, and, therefore, pot is good, so everybody should smoke pot if it helps you.

Always on Friday, he picks up his two daughters for the weekend. This started back in 1973 while separated, then 1974 the divorce, and it's 1977 now. Daddy always took them to a fun place: the beach, the pool, had picnics with

Mother, the family, and friends at the parks. A fun time is had by all. His actions speak louder than words, but when he is with his little girls, he tells them how good the Father, Jesus, and his Holy Spirit are. If anything important comes up, his lovely mother would keep his girls. He was raised on Christ's love from the day he was baptized! When the Holy Spirit comes into your heart and mind, you know that you know that you know. A great love that comes from knowing and next to knowing is knowing where to find out. The Father's love is put in your heart and mind; it's just too good like lightning running thru your veins. It brings you to your knees with joy and happiness. You have no doubts. God's Spirit is real, and Jesus is God who saved us humans from death. With Christ, you have eternal life, and your soul is in the Father's thoughts forever, living in God's holy thoughts.

He meets more people in the drug trade and makes more money in three days. He quits his job and goes in hook, line, and sinker; but he brings in the love of Jesus the Christ of God with him. He tells everyone in a kind and loving way what they are doing is wrong, that they should make sure they have Christ Jesus in their hearts and minds, and to read their Bible, to get one if they do not have one. Freddy does have a plan to go to school after he makes over $50,000 to pay for school, room, board, and car. His first big deal is selling twenty-five pounds at one time to one man from New York City in the end of 1977, and there is a middleman who have to have his cut. He is meeting people from all walks of life and from different cities in Florida and all big cities all around the USA; people are flying in. The problem is Freddy trusts all he meets so he makes money, but then he trusts the people he meets too much he gets ripped off a lot; he so much would like to see the good in man. One good deal pays off; one bad deal so he is not getting ahead. It's good he has a low overhead.

He moves into a house with a two-car garage. He has the good life, family, friends, parties, sex with all kinds of beautiful girls. There are a few girls who were special. He thinks about having a son with one of them one day. It will be nice. He loves his daughters, but a son will be nice.

After about five months of nonstop fun and giving money away to help others, he believes this is a good thing, and he's not seeing the dark side, hurting souls. He wants to open a health food store. He's always been in that state of mind, be healthy. Plus he works out at the gym four days a week. Being healthy is the way to be.

He rents a warehouse that is twenty feet across, eighty feet from front door to the big warehouse door in the back that open to the road. There is a bathroom at the end on the right, a big empty warehouse. He's across from a football and baseball fields and tennis and basketball courts; so he thinks it's a great spot for a health food store.

He builds the inside from scratch. Everything has to pass a city coed from the kitchen to the sign out front that reads "The Nature Center." Eve, she is perfect, this girl, soft silky white skin, a pleaser to lie next to, perfect body, and lovely face for sure. This is what Adam has in the garden. She paints the sign by hand; she is from another country going to art school here in beautiful Fort Lauderdale, Florida, where the fun never stops.

He makes the bar four feet high by six feet wide, then turns right two feet. It's all wood with the top covered with all kinds of pictures of healthy-looking people, animals, and nature. Each picture has to be covered with a thin coat of glue and let it dry for seven hours. After the first coat of epoxy on top of the wooden bar has dried off, he glues the pictures and waits for twenty-four hours and then puts the next four coats of epoxy on top. The bar has a canopy over it so the dust will not fall into the liquid epoxy while drying, but the epoxy will create bubbles in the liquid that you have to use a torch and lightly go over the bubble to get them to pop out.

After fixing the plumbing, electrical lights, camera action, the store is open, and most of the people are not into healthy food or protein drinks at that time, so the business is very slow. He has T-shirts made as well. He also creates an all-natural snow cone and calls it South Florida Snow. The money coming in by selling pot is a little more than working weekly. So he spends time at the beach to get the perfect tan. He goes to the finest men's store; he is in a play-boy state of mind, but he does not buy a fancy car; he keeps it low-key. The Lord has given him enough rope to hang himself.

You know how time goes by fast. Well, living the fast life goes by even quicker. Freddy eventually makes his first big mistake by going out of town to help a friend. Not going into details, but he would have had the money to quiet this negative living and go to school, but he has ended up in the Orlando city jail with a $100,000 bond to get out, and back then in 1978, that was a lot of money to a small-time pot dealer.

When the dawn breaks, the paperwork is over, and he is being led into his cell at the time the big story of the day is on the TV; his pot bust of two thousand pounds at a small airport is a stone's throw from the city of Orlando. All seventeen inmates give him a great welcome. He's the coolest one in this cell because he is on TV. On his first night there, he borrows a

Bible from one of his cellmates and opens it up to Luke 17: "Then said he unto the disciples, it is impossible that offences will come: but woe unto him, through whom they come" (Jesus)!

Pop! He's mind is opened, and he sees. He is the tempter by selling pot! You see, it's not the sinner that's bad; it's the person that temps the person to sin. That's the bad person. He breaks down in a cry and asks the Father for forgiveness, which he does. The next day, he asks for his own Bible that was in his room at the hotel. He gets it by the other person who got busted with him, his family member.

Freddy tells the men he thinks this deal feels like his buyers are fake, but the money is luring them in. There are four persons involved in the bust. Two will get out the next day; one of them owned the pot. Freddy does not have the money to make bail, so he passes the time by reading his Bible every day. He gets a lawyer, a local one. He hopes he knows the system and he can get out of first-time offense with no jail time. Got to get out of this city jail.

There are all kinds of crimes men have committed in the big cell of twenty men. To kill time, he plays chess with the men who know how and lets them know the love and forgiveness God has for his children. By his actions and reading his Bible every day, the men get to know he is a true believer. When you have Jesus, you have the Holy Spirit, and you have the Father's love, and what a wonderful love it is. "I and my Father are One" (John 10:30).

After the state lowers his bond to $10,000, he can bond out with his sister's help. But on his last day in jail, the thirtieth day, you see, he never played checkers at all while he was there. He is challenged to play against the best checkers player in the cell, who is undefeated. At first, Freddy says no, that he does not play that game, but then he does, and in less than thirty minutes, he beats the best. The black man can't believe it; he asks for a replay. Freddy says no, but the man bags him, telling him he needs another game.

"Okay!" Freddy says. Freddy beats him again, and he tells him God is within me, and to make sure he is within you. All the men are blown away that the best player lost to a man who never played the game. Freddy is let out and goes home to loved ones.

The health food store has been locked up; everything has been sitting for over a month. The biggest money-making deal is a bust, and all that's left is paying off all bills with very little money in the shoebox. The Holy Spirit gives him a way out before the bust, but all the money to be made pulls him in. Plus he is going to go to helicopter school to have a future. He's back in the house; then he borrows money to pay the rent for a year in advance for the nature center store when he knows he will be going to jail. He needs to make money to pay for it all, so he must sell his car and other items. Only the family knows of the bust in Orlando, so he still has his connection. Deep down in his heart, the Holy Spirit is pulling him back to the fold, and he sees how he is hurting souls by selling pot. Pot helps him, but it might not help others that have dyslexia. Only time will tell if marijuana is helpful for others. This is the Christ of the Father speaking.

I *am* the true vine, **and** Father is the husbandman, "garner." Every branch in me that bringth **not** fruit he takes away: and every branch that bares fruit, he purgeth it, that it may beareth more fruit. Abide in me, and I in you. As the branch cannot bear fruit of itself, except it abide in the vine; no more can you except you abide in me. I am the vine, you are the branches: He that abideth in me, and I in him, the same bringth more fruit: For without me you can do nothing. If a man abide not in me, he is cast forth as a branch and is withered; and men gather them, and cast them into a fire, and they are burned. If you abide in me, and my words abide in you, you shall ask what you will, and it shall be done unto you. Here in is my Father glorified, that you bare much fruit: so, shall you be my disciples. As the Father has loved me, so have I loved you: continue you in my love. If you keep my commandments, you shall abide in my love; even as I have keep my Fathers commandments, and abide in his love. These things have I spoken unto you, that my joy might remain in you, and that your joy might be full." (John 15:11)

He has made some money, and all is going well. Then one of his friends betrays him and steals 350 pounds of pot from his garage when he was out with all the kids. With his two daughters and his sister's three kids, he would drive the VW with the top down on the car and play music the Moody Blues or Beatles; they were off to a park and the ice cream store. Freddy was told by the Holy Spirit three times not to trust this man, but he gave him his trust. The Holy Spirit is always right!

Now he reports to the owner of the pot and takes his life savings with him all he had, to show he was broken into and the pot was stolen. He tells him what happened and gives him the money. Two days go by, and Freddy does not know that the man he got it from got the pot from another man, and that man sent over, to the nature center three men. The men beat Freddy up, and after that they ask him a question. He tells them the truth, but they do not believe him. They think he set up the rip-off and made lots more money. The men tell Freddy to give them the money, or he's a dead man! They take Freddy to a hotel, and he is pushed into the room. In the back by the window is a glow, and he walks to it. The very big Bible is open, and his eyes are fixed on one passage. He reads the words that stand out: "Fear not, for I am with you; Be not dismayed, for I am your God. I will strengthen you, yes, I will help you, I will uphold you with my righteous right hand" (Isaiah 41:10).

He turns around, and the gun is pointing at him. He doesn't say a word. Then the three men look at each other, like a power of truth has come over them, and one says, "We believe you!" Then the other two say, "Yes! We believe too." The Holy Spirit has put the truth in their minds these three men are given the truth, and they believe Freddy did not ripe them off. Then one man takes out the bullet from the gun, gives it to Freddy, and says, "This is a reminder of how close you were from death." On the drive home, the head guy tells Freddy he needs a thousand dollars in cash so they can fly back home. Freddy makes a quick call to borrow it from his very close friends. Praise is to Jesus! Saved again! Our heavenly Father has all the pieces of his life planned. He has a calling that only he is assigned to do.

Months go by, and a person gives Freddy money he owed him. Another month goes by, and it turns out that one of the men in the Orlando bust got busted again flying in fifty pounds of cocaine, and all the past came to the future. And in a blink of an eye, Freddy's in Macon Georgia with his new lawyer who got all of Freddy's money, and there in a courthouse with other lawyers and men who were busted. They all are tied to one South American big drug lord named Escobar. Freddy only did the one deal, so he knows no one but the men in his Orlando bust. After the first day is over, Freddy's lawyer is good. He's a middle-aged man with smarts; he gets Freddy to meet the judge who will preside over all the cases. Which Freddy is a very small link in the chain? He comes in the judge's chambers with his lawyer, and the judge says in a deep Southern voice, pointing his finger to the chair right in front of his desk, "Have a seat, son." Freddy sits down, and the judge asks him, "What do you have to say for yourself?" The words flow out of Freddy's mouth without thinking:

"'Forgive a man even in his sin, for that is semblance of divine love, and that is the highest love on earth'" (Gilbert Hay).

There is silence in the room for about seven seconds. Then the judge says, "Send this man to Eglin!" The judge stands up. Then everybody stands up. He says again, "Send this man to Eglin!" The judge tells one man to get the phone and call Elgin! Another man talks to the judge in his ear. Freddy moves toward his lawyer and whispered, "What's Eglin?" "Oh! You will like it there!" The man on the phone calls the lawyer over, and they talk for a few minutes. The judge talks to Freddy's lawyer, then Freddy, and his lawyer, both of them walk out of the judge's chambers. They walk out of the court-house and take a cab to the hotel where the law-yer tells Freddy he must report in two weeks to Eglin, and that night in the hotel room, Freddy is told all he will do to get ready to start serving time in Eglin in two weeks. Plus his state bust will run concurrent with the federal crime, even though Freddy had nothing to do with flying pounds of cocaine into the United States.

Two weeks pass, and he is in a plane flying to Eglin Air Force Base to check in for a nine-month get away from the rat race, of the noise of the world, and, after his nine months, two-year probation. What he hears from his lawyer is that all the men in his bust in Orlando got twelve years in a tougher prison and five years' probation. The Father has saved his hide again.

He checks in, and his first two weeks are in an old wooden house, which is all open inside and has fans on the ceiling, old not very good beds, something the military had back in World War II. The bathroom is in the middle, and the place does not have heat or an air conditioner, open windows in summer, shut in winter.

On his third day, a nice-looking young man walks up to him and says, "Hello, my name is Michael."

"Hello, my name is Freddy."

"You will like it here." He hands him a book. "Thank you, Michael." He looks down at the book, and when he looks up, Michael is gone. The title of the book is *Wisdom of the Spiritual Heart*. He sits down on his bunk and looks through every interesting page with a thought and a beautiful drawing on each page. He'll be reading this book with his little book and his Bible each night. Even though he looks each day for Michael, he never sees him again.

He is in the county club of prisons. Two weeks have passed, and he is assigned to building 3, sections 3B1. He thinks, *Three B one, Father, Son, and Holy Spirit are one. That's cool.*

He is so happy to get in this building, and he thanks the Father God.

Inside this place in the middle are the bathrooms and showers. Then divided into four big sections are twenty-five cubicles, four feet by eight feet, with a bed, desk with storage on top; and on both sides of the desk are cabinets about five feet tall, one to hang clothes, the other shelves for whatever. This is a space in the heated and air-conditioned building. Ninety percent of the men here have committed a crime with drugs without guns involved. Most are first-time offenders like Freddy, and if you do anything stupid here, you're sent out ASAP to a not-so-nice prison. Who knows where. This is the country club of prisons. There is no place better than this to do your time for your crime. Anything from sixth grade to college, were school course given here. There were possibilities of learning anything at the country club.

On his first Sunday, Freddy meets with the chaplain. He's a Spanish Catholic priest, a believer in Christ, and it shows in his actions. Freddy lets him know he would like to get involved with the church. Two weeks later, he is asked if he would like to be part of the newspaper that's put out once a month called *The Doin' Times*. He will write church news and, on the spiritual side of life, thoughts from the Bible, the little book, and the new book *Wisdom of the Spiritual Heart*.

Every morning at seven, he is to report to the landscaping supervisor, who puts on a not-so-happy-to-see-you face. Freddy is assigned to take care of the warden's and assistant warden's homes. Each day, they drive out by truck with all the tools to the warden's homes and other homes in the same area. Each man is dropped off to take care of his section. What is cool is they have riding lawn mowers. The front is small, but the back is huge.

They pull up to the front of the warden's home. It's nice because it's shaded with trees along the road. The front yard grass is nicely made. The driveway is covered with leaves. Facing the road from the front door looking out, you can see on the other side of the road there are three more homes that are not as nice.

Each home occupies a small acre, but the lawns are the same for one man; it's big and there's lots to do.

In the backyard of the warden's home, there's an open patio and lots of shade trees. The gulf ocean washes up seaweed to shore, but the place is big and beautiful. Doing time here is very peaceful. You're on your own get the work done, and no one bothers you. The man who works next to Freddy is named Jonathan, and he takes care of the home next to the assistant warden's home. It's just as nice.

At 11:45, they drive back to the prison for lunch. It's in an old building, but the food is great! It is cooked by prisoners who like to cook, and the new cafeteria building is almost done. Then he goes back to work at 1:00 till 3:30, then goes back to the shop, unloads the truck, and cleans the tools; and workday is over at four o'clock. Now time is his; and he goes to the gym, walks down to the lake, or just sits on a bench and enjoys Mother Nature. When he would sit down by the lake, birds would put on a show by flying out of the tree to skim across the water, then back up to another tree. Dinner is from 5:00 till 7:00, but they can sit in the dining area till 7:30.

During the second week of working with Jonathan, he shows Freddy a getaway place in the woods; it's on the side that Freddy oversees. They walk on a path into the woods, then into a very quiet and peaceful undeveloped area with logs to sit on. He is offered a hit off a very thinly rolled joint, but he refuses it and says, "I need a break from pot, thank you." They talk for about ten minutes how they got there, their age, and where they live. Then they go back to work.

It is mandatory to singing with men in the church choir for two days a week if you want to go out of the prison, once a month on Sunday. The man gets to leave the prison and the air base and go out to other churches in the city, sing songs, and have a great dinner and conversation with other believers. That was always fun.

It is Freddy's second month in prison. On the job in the morning, there in the quiet place, Jonathan gives Freddy a very thin rolled joint. Freddy says, "No, thanks, at first," but Jonathan says, "I've been here for over two years. It's okay. They can't test you for pot! Only for alcohol. Just don't drink or fight with anyone, and you'll be all right here." They start the day in a happy state of mind. A thin joint in this prison costs lots. The $.50 an hour becomes $3.50 a day. He puts it in his account. He buys fruits and other items from the little store in the prison—no money no honey. Of course, there is the trading of items in this prison.

That week, Freddy is called to the counselor office. He's not sure why. It might be because he smoked pot; he's a little frightened. In the counselor's office, he tells Freddy he must go home for one week, then report back at Elgin to finish his time there. This is what all men must do who have six months left before they are released from this prison. Freddy is relieved but does not like the idea of going home when he has little time to do. So he takes advantage of the time away and makes plans to bring in an ounce of pot not to sell just to have for himself and friends. Marijuana affects him differently than most people because of his dyslexia; it helps him to read. Freddy has the love, joy, enlightened state of mind, of who Christ Jesus is. From all his experience in his life, when he was a baby and his mind was opened after baptism, the bubble of love, his search for Christ, the 30 day fast at Johnathan Dickerson State Park, Getting closer to the Father, and how he was shown the truth about the Moody Blues. The one thing he knows for sure is God never leaves you or forsakes you because of your sin. If you ask for forgiveness with a sincere heart and he knows you, he remembers your sin no more, but does not mean you get away with the crime.

When he smokes, he reads better, and he works harder, and he is always thinking of God the Father, Jesus, and the Holy Spirit. If you're around him, he'll tell you about the love of Jesus and how to be saved.

The week home goes by fast, and he makes his pot connection, and he is flying back to the Elgin airport not far from the prison. It's dark, and after 10:00 p.m., the man who picks him up smokes pot and is given a small amount of it for his help. He drives Freddy to the area where the quiet place is, but the other side of where

the woods started is where the air force people live in their own homes or trailers. He gets
out of the car and walks into the woods to the
quiet place, and he puts the pot in a little tin
box and puts it in the hole in the ground where
he dug before he left, then the wire mesh on top
then cover with leaves; it's a safe place. He walks
back to the car, and then they drive back to the
prison. He checks into the front office like it's a
school dorm, where he takes a urine test. That
night, he sleeps in the old house before he's able
to get back to his four-by-eight-feet cubicle 3B1
for the next six months.

In the first week back, he does not go near
the quiet place. The next week he goes in but
does not go near the area where the pot is, but
in the third week, he does and rolls fat joint,
puts the pot back in the safe place, and calls
Jonathan over to share a smoke. The joint is
fatter, and Jonathan sees that. Freddy cuts it in
half and thanks him for being a friend and says,
"A good deed is never lost, he who sows curtsy,
reaps friendship. He who plants kindness gathers love." Then he tells him on his week home

he picks up some money, so he buys some pot from one of the men inside the prison. This is Thanksgiving month, and we need to be thankful of all of God's blessing. It's not the truth, on how he got the pot, but he does not want anyone to know he has an ounce of pot in the ground, word of mouth goes through the prison like a dried-up Christmas tree on fire. They leave the quiet place and start their work with an open mind. You know that this is what Eve ate in the garden to open her mind. This is what Freddy believes, but if you are only thinking on Christ Jesus, is it bad?

At the end of the month, he's call to the office to talk to the counselor. He is told he will be flying with chains on his feet and hands on a small plane to Orlando to get the state charge to run concurrent with his federal charge, part of the deal his lawyer made for Freddy. One week later, he is in chains on a six-seated plane to Orlando with one other prisoner. That same day, he is in court, and it runs together with the federal time. But they do not fly him back; he's put in the Orlando city jail with seventeen men in one cell with one urinal, one toilet, two showers side by side. Each day, two man clean the cell floor and bathroom area, and in twelve days, it will be Freddy's turn. He reads the newspaper each day to pass the very boring time. After the third day, he realizes how blessed he really has it at Elgin. It's five days before Christmas. He has been here for almost two weeks. He finally asks the Lord for help and falls to sleep in a dream the Holy Spirit tells him what to tell the officer that brings the mail. So the next day, he tells her what the Holy Spirit has told him, and the next day, he is on a plane back to Elgin, and it's two days before Christmas. Praise the Lord Jesus! The Christ of God! His friends ask him what happened!!!! He is happy to tell them the story of being in hell and the love of the Lord that got him out and back to the country club.

Back on the job, lucky to have the same area back, he is out in the open air, and in God's creation, it's gorgeous—the heavens, earth, and sea; it's all too beautiful. The thought comes to mind out of the little book.

"Love all God's creation, both the whole, and every grain of sand. Love every leaf, every ray of light, love all the animals, love the plant, love each thing, if you love each thing you will precede the mystery of God in all" (Dostoevsky).

The landscapers do not leave the base when they go to work because the warden and staff live not far from the prison. The country club, that is. So when the men come back from work, they are never searched. Who would think that someone would have pot in the warden's house.

Pot smokers from the sixties and seventies will understand what I'm about to tell you. Others condemn, but the Father has forgiven! His Son died for us on the cross.

He has been gone for over two weeks, and the pot is just sitting in the ground, and he is so happy to be back in the open air with the Father's nature like being on a camping trip here at Eglin.

In this prison, you get to know people fast. There are not so many souls here, and so Freddy challenges twenty-one of his friends whom they have gotten to know, the ones who like to smoke pot. His challenge is a volleyball game, eleven men on a side. Best two out of three wins a delightful surprise. Freddy picks his team, and Jonathan picks his men. They both talk about this game while working together after Freddy got back from hell in the Orlando jail. Freddy talks with Johnathan in the secret place to put this fun time together. The teams are picked, and they're playing on nice white soft sand, just like on the beach. It's not far from the building where they live. There are no surveillance cameras watching them on the beach area.

The game begins, and Freddy's team takes the lead. They win twenty-one to nine. Thinking they will win the next game, they take it easy at first, and before they know it, they lose, at twenty-one to nineteen.

Now before the third game, Freddy shows every one what they're playing for; he has the goods. They're not thin joints, so the stakes are high to get high and walk away with one. Freddy tells everyone that only the winners will get a joint. He tells them that so the game will be to the best goes the fruit of their labor. Freddy hits the first serve over the net, and it gets hit back. The game begins. They take the lead. Then for the next hour, it's a battle for the right to get an open mind, to think deeper and clearer if you only smoke a little. The battle goes on for another half hour of overtime, and Freddy's team loses. His men are sad as he hands out eleven joints to Jonathan and his fearless men.

Freddie's team, who fought hard, are so disappointed and looking on as each man gets his reward. But wait! A surprise. He pulls out another ten joints and gives them to his men and tells all twenty-one men no one is going home empty-handed this day. Everyone cheers. Then he tells them, "Please make sure you get right with God, and get to know Christ Jesus while you're in here, because out in the world, lots of temptation will come at you. You need him so he can help fight off the arrows of the devil, which are those lures in the sea of life. To know and feel his love, it's all to beautiful. You'll be happy for the rest of your days on earth. Please be safe with your winnings." An enjoyable time is had by all! No one ever got busted

Weeks later, some of the men who played tells him they are going to church, and they are reading their Bibles; the seed has been planted.

What Freddy and his two closest friends do before he flies to Orlando is in the evening once a week, they cut up fruits. They make a supersalad with apples, oranges nectarines, bananas, watermelon, pears, and raisins with honey poured over the top, and it's chilled on ice in a bucket for half an hour. So they take a walk; they have so much freedom for being in a prison. It was like living in an all-male college dorm, just like back in 4H days. Outside the four buildings that look alike, the sidewalk goes all around, and throughout the camp, the sidewalks are eight feet wide, and when you pass the little church, it leads to the building where the wardens and staff offices were.

The back area going out to the lake, there are no lights and no cameras, but there are lots of trees. You get the feeling you're in a national state park on a camping trip, and you have the freedom to go anytime after work, and you have weekends off. Only the cooks and kitchen help have weird hours.

After the walk, coming back with the munchies, someone would pull the plastic container out, turn it over, and then put back on ice. They let the juices of the fruit and honey drip back down. Then Freddy would say a prayer. Then they pull the bucket out of the ice open the lid each one filled their bowls with the fruit of God's love, all covered with honey. They are so aware of how God has blessed them, to be doing time for their crime in this prison.

Christmas is over, and the new year is just in. He gets back on his workout routine after work each day. At nights, he works on the article that will go in the *Doin' Times* paper, and weekends are for church obligation. Each month goes by pretty much the same. He's down to one month left, and another miracle has happened, but that will be kept a secret for now. He cannot forget all the miracles the Lord has done for him.

The plans are when he gets home he will move in with his ex-wife to help with the kids and get back on his feet. In June 1980, the day of Freddy's release, he is given a $100 let out the doors where he checked in nine months ago. It was like being in mother's belly, very peaceful and now being reborn into the world. He has a new book: *Wisdom of the Spiritual Heart*, and with more faith in Christ Jesus, lots more faith. His mother pays the airfare for his one-way trip back home.

# Chapter 6

❊

## Every Good Boy Deserves Favor

"There our times that I have found the
truth, times I know I am wrong!"

He is picked up at the airport by his mother,
brother, and two sisters. Two of the kids are still
in school. The house only has two bedrooms
and two bathrooms. They are all happy Freddy
is out of prison, but only he knows it was the
country club. He knows Jesus has saved him
again. He's so blessed; he did a crime, and the
Father still gave him an easy time. Thank you,
Father, is it because Freddy gave up everything!
Father, mother, brother, sister, wife, son, and
daughters to seek Jesus on his walk back in 1973,
in search of the Christ of God, who knows his

heart. "Better a heart filled with Christ love then a mind filled with knowledge."

After a week at his mother's home, he moves over to his ex-wife's house. She tells him she needs help with the children; she has one more from her second marriage, a cute three-year-old girl. He gets a part-time job so he can be home for the kids when they get out of school and day care. Two weeks have passed. Life is going well. He comes home from picking up the girls on a Friday, and there is a note on the TV that reads, "Freddy, I cannot take the pressure anymore. Take care of the girls and take or sell whatever is left in the house. I'll call you, Brinda." He turns his head, looking at the girls playing without a care in the world. He calls his mother and tells her the situation, and she tells him, "You and the girls can move in with us." He has his two daughters and another three-year-old girl. He treats the new daughter as his own. He packs their suitcases for a couple of days, and he'll be back to get the rest on the weekend. He has no car, but he has asked a friend to pick him up and take them over to his mother's house. Freddy with the three girls are living in the Florida room/laundry room, and the girls sleep on a folded bed, while Freddy sleeps on the sofa. He quit the job that is close to his ex-wife's house and gets one that is close to his mother's house so he can ride a bike to work. His day starts by getting the girls up and in the bathroom, then some breakfast. Then they are off to school by bus. He'd walk the youngest to the day care up the road, maybe five blocks, then back home and get on the bike off to his work. He is working in a store that when you walk in the scent gets you into a "gotta eat" mood. The place sells kitchen items, wine, food, and a deli in the back of the store where you could get lunch. Coming home from work, he'd pick up the one at the day care first. Then the others get off the bus. Daddy takes all the children to the park each day after school, and on the weekends, they would go to the beach or the pool at the hotel on the beach, where he would teach them all to swim. Six months have gone by, and he still has not gotten any word from his ex-wife, but the girls are happy with Daddy.

It's been a good year now, and he still receives no word from the girls' mother. He gets a lawyer so he can get custody of all the girls. It takes months, and his court date is three days away. The next night, he gets a call from the ex-wife telling him she has gotten a fantastic job, and the kids will be able to go to a private school. She tells him an exceptional story, and she goes on and on, but now she can only take the littlest one; she can only take the other two when they finish the school year. She tells all that to him, and it sounds so good for the children. He knows it would be years before he could get the kids out of his mother's house or anything as nice as that. He prays on it and believes the girls are best off with their mother, and she calls days before the court date. Plus he can start working on getting out of his mother's house. With what he pays for the day care, he can get a cheap car. As soon as school year ends, she picks them up, and they're off to the Cayman Islands with their mother. He stays in touch with the girls by phone. About a month later, a friend gets him back into construction, to do carpenter work for forty hours a week, making good hourly money. Construction is back on the upside. He still rides his bike for two miles to his friend's house. They use his car to go to the job site. Freddy still has the Nature Center store, but it's been closed—no money, no honey. People are not even interested in smoothies or health food products yet. Freddy is riding his bike everywhere he goes. He is in great shape, and he gets a good tan working under the Florida sun.

He is out of prison for three years now, and so much has happened in his life, but God steps in, in a *big* way in 1982. It's like one man's heaven is another man's hell. Freddy with almost all the new people he meets, and he wants to find out if they are spiritual thinkers or whether they believe in God, if they know Christ Jesus. If not, then he tells the person about the love of the Father through his Christ—how he is real, how he is always there to provide whatever you need; and sometimes his great love, a surprise of extraordinary joy, unspeakable joy fills your heart. He explains it like this: it's not a religion but a personal walk with the Creator of the universe. Freddy knows this because of his walk to Daytona Beach and the pouring of his love into his heart on the seventh day ten years ago. He shares how the voice told him that Jesus is God on earth!—you can take it to the bank!

It's Tuesday morning at work, and he meets Al, one of the new men who started working for the construction company on Monday. It's Al's second day on the job site. Before the work starts, Freddy asks Al, "Do you believe in God?" In a loud voice, Al says, "God is bullshit. There is no God!" Freddy tries to help him to understand the truth about the personal relationship with the Creator of the universe and Yasha Jesus, the Christ of the Father, and his love for all mankind; but after the third time, he tells Freddy, "God is all bullshit, man! I don't want to hear about God anymore."

"A fool says in his heart there is no God."

They must work together for today, so Freddy tells him he will not talk about it anymore. Freddy and Al starts nailing in the rat runs on the underside of the truss. This is to steady the truss, so, on the next day, the men can walk on the top of the tress. You will have to move fast but careful not to move the truss too much, while you walk on them caring a sheet of plywood over your head to lay it down on top of truss. That's why the rat runs are done first, so the truss doesn't bow too much.

They are walking inside of the truss, which is about eight feet above the floor, to the middle, and start working. They just finish the room, and it's break time. After break time, they get started on the next room, and then the horn blows for lunch. Al goes home, and his girlfriend has baked a cake for his birthday. He's twenty-one today. "You say it's your birthday? Well! Happy birthday to ya." Beaties. In that half-hour lunch, Freddy eats his homemade lunch, then takes a fifteen-minute nap on a sheet of plywood. Freddy wakes up, and the whistle blows. All of them go back to work. Lunch goes by quick in a nap dream. Al comes back fifteen minutes late, smiling. He must have gotten some Tuesday afternoon delight. They do not talk. They just start working together. Thirty minutes after, Al gets back, and all hell breaks loose.

Now lesson to this carefully, Freddy has the nail gun, and the young Al is holding the l"x1" piece of wood, it's eight feet long called a firing strip. The job was call putting in the rat runs. Al has come to the end of the firing strip of wood and steps over the truss in front of him, going slowly, then turns around and comes back and steps on the truss. He steps over, and it breaks like a toothpick. Then all the trusses behind Al go down as Al falls fast to the cemented floor. All this happens in seconds, and the stack of plywood that was sitting on top of the truss at the northeast corner of the building flies just past Freddy' feet. As he steps back one truss, holding onto the top of the truss, the plywood hits the floor. It shakes the whole building, breaking the truss loose from the wall where they first started. Freddy thinks what they have already nailed will hold him if he stays still. He thinks he is safe but no! He's not looking behind him. He is looking for the kid who fell. What's happening behind him are the trusses falling in a domino effect right at Freddy. All the trusses are coming at him; he does not even know it, but quicker than a blink of the eye, he feels hands, grabs his hands, and pulls them off the truss. As they're apart, he feels a hand pushing on his back just enough so now he is falling and hits the cement with his feet, then a slip onto his butt right next to the stack of plywood, which is about three feet in height. The truss followed him down, tapping the top of his head, then hitting the stack of plywood with a big bang! This stops from hitting and killing Freddy, but at the same moment, he hears the sound of someone's breath coming out from under the stack of plywood. He turns his head to look, and it's Al's face with eyes wide open. Freddy wiggles his way out from under the broken truss and yells for help. Workers are coming in with car jacks and jack up the stack of plywood so it's not on top of the boy. Freddy is still in the only place where he is saved. Thanking God for saving him again, he feels the hands of God or an angel. It's a miracle he's not broken into pieces or dead.

Less than five minutes, the ambulance is on the job site. Then the paramedic rushes into action. They give Al a shot of something first, then bring him out from under the eight-hundred pounds of plywood that the men jacked up seven minutes earlier. They do everything they could. One man says to the other, "He is gone." Freddy was saved by the hands of God; the push that had him fall to the ground landing next to the plywood. He has witnessed to young Al, but he refused three times to hear about the Christ of the Father. Jesus did say, "Very, very I say unto you, before Abraham was, I am" (John 8:58). He feels very sad for Al, knowing he will stand in front of God without the love of Jesus in his heart, with no wedding clothes on. Freddy keeps this miracle to himself as they head to the hospital, Al in the ambulance; Freddy rides in a car driven by a friend. He's not hurt but must get check out. He wants to praise God, out loud, and tell everyone how he was saved, but he keeps it inside. Al is dead, and his mother and girlfriend come in crying as they look at his cold lifeless body. Freddy is checked out and released. He keeps the miracle to himself and just tells his family when his mother comes home from work. She heard about it on the radio news on her drive home from work. She gives her son a big hug and kisses.

He is back to work the next day. Early in the morning, he walks past the room where the accident was. He sees men from the truss company cutting up the truss and throwing them into a truck to destroy the evidence the trusses were faulty. He is not going to sue anyone, anyway, but weeks later, he does feel a light pain in his lower back but puts it out of his mind, and he keeps working. He's riding his bike everywhere and still goes to the gym—same routine of life going by.

Then one day at work, he picks up two cylinder blocks. He does not use his knees but bends over with his back. Then the disc that is hurting in his back pops; the L5 disk blows out, and pain shoots through the body down the legs and up to the brain. You got pain here, got pain! After working another week, the pain is still nagging at him, so he sets up an appointment with workman's comp. After seeing them getting X-rays, he's on leave from construction work but stays with the company getting leeds for new construction work for about three months for the company. The pain from the bulging disk gets worse in the next months.

He then sets up an appointment with a lawyer to start the lawsuit on the truss company. He used the same one that Al's mother has gotten, and the lawyer turns out to throw them both under the bus. Freddy, being very trustful in all that the lawyer tells him, signs the papers that hurt his case and his closing statements are very damaging to the outcome of the trial. Freddy can't believe what he hears. Freddy loses his case. After the trial is over and days of roiling things over in his mind, he believes the lawyer wanted to lose he got paid by all the parties on the other side.

Frederick Haussman views the scene of the accident, where he suffered minor injuries.

Roof collapse turns birthday joy to grief
By Michael Romano
Staff Writer

At noontime Wednesday, Albert Elrod enjoyed one of the happiest moments of his life—a quiet luncheon celebration to mark his 21st birthday, complete with a frosted chocolate cake baked by his bride-to-be, Patty Marra.

Less than two hours later, Elrod was dead, crushed by a huge stack of plywood that dropped from an unfinished roof at a construction site outside Pompano Beach.

Al's mother and Freddy get nothing from the truss company. The truth is the truss broke when stepped on. It was a faulty truss that caused the accident and killed the boy. But God saved Freddy! Bottom line is he is blessed he is alive with all body parts working, but a pain in the lower back.

Another year goes by, and Brinda loses her job in the Cayman's, and she and the girls are back to living in Boca. Freddy is happy to see the girls and spends two months with them before Brinda moves up north. Now he can only see them in the summer.

The good part of Freddy's life now is he got a job in the T-shirt business not far from the Nature Center store, so he sleeps there for now. It is centrally located for riding the bicycle. He learns all about the business in the coming months, and he likes that it brings out his creative abilities.

His workman's comp clam which now has two parts; one is medical which you cannot settle by law for now, and the other is work ability. Can you work at all? He learns a lot from the T-shirt company, but they can't pay him a higher wage. He sells one item at the store. This one item can tell you more about Freddy's life, but the story does not need to be about Freddy's life but your life. Where are you in your life? Are you getting closer to the Christ of the Father Yasha, Jesus the Christ of God? You do not have to believe me, but you need to believe in Jesus.

With the money from the one item he sold and a load from a bank, he buys a beautiful new 750cc motorcycle the Honda Shadow. So he can get a job as head man at a head shop/T-shirt company out west in Davie. After he gets the job and has worked for three months, a friend is moving out of his one-bedroom apartment in the city of Oakland Park. The rent is low, so he moves out of the store and into the apartment. Every night after riding on his motorcycle, he cleans the bike first, then brings it in the apartment. Overnight, he keeps it in the living room. It's a good-looking bike, and he likes to keep it that way. After a year, he gets very creative and puts ideas on shirts but keeps them to himself. He is fading away from reading his Bible every night, and getting into dating as many girls as he can. From eighteen to fifty, the ladies love the man on the cool bike; he gives them all a nice ride.

Then three big breaks come his way. First one, he creates a T-shirt design for a very popular FM rock and roll radio morning show. The T-shirt is called the sleazy weasel T-shirt. It sells from Homestead to West Palm Beach, and it sells like hotcakes. He must buy a SUV to deliver all the shirts to the places that would like to sell them.

The second is, his lawyer from the workman comp case calls him and tells him that workman's comp would like to settle on part of his claim, but the medical cannot be settled by law, for now. Now he has money in the bank, and that leads to number three. There is a house that goes up for sale on his block; the elderly lady died, and her husband died years earlier. Freddy checks it out with the relator and sees it has a big backyard with six oranges trees and one grapefruit tree, seven all together in bad shape; and the last orange tree the one in the far back looks dead. With challenging work, this could become beautiful. He buys the house and signs a one-year contract with the radio station. He has his first back operation. It is the new advance way to operate, going in with a very thin hose and sucking out the disk that is pushing on the nerves, but leaving in some of the L5disk, you know the cushion between the bones in your back. The operation was such a success he feels no pain. God is blessing him in a big way, and there is more on the way.

After papers are signed, the house is his, and the banks. Freddy starts working the front yard first. He gets busy pulling weeds, dead old bushes with rope that's tied to the SUV he pulls out. He cleans and puts the big stepping-stones that reach the driveway up to the front porch in a neater alignment. Then he plants a tree that just came out of its seed in the middle of the front yard and puts in flowers by the newly made of logs sign with the address numbers in gold for his house. The front is finish. For now, he has no pain in his lower back because his back operation was a remarkable success.

The T-shirt sales are up. Everyone at the radio station are happy, and Freddy is busy. Now the big backyard only on the weekend does he works on the fruit trees. They are in very bad condition; the leaves are covered with black dirt that does not just wash off with just squirting water, because years of the sun baking the dirt on them. The trees bark has a fungus on it from top to bottom, and most branches. With the Moody Blues playing in the background, he starts with the tree that is closest to the back door of the house. He climbs to the top of the tree with a bucket of water with a hook to hang off, and with a rag, he cleans each leaf by hand, then, with a hand brush, scrubs off the fungus on the bark. It took over four hours cleaning it all. Then he sprayed off the whole tree with a hard spray of water.

He digs up the ground in a four-foot ring around the base of the tree and throws that dirt in a pile away from the tree. Then he puts good dirt mixed with fertilizer around the tree's roots, and fertilized the ground at the base of the tree, hoping for some miracle growth. It took seven hours of arduous work with no pain throughout the body. He will clean one tree each weekend, even the last tree in the far back, that one that looks dead, only had fifteen leaves on it. It looks so dead you can push it over. It's the last one in the very back of the yard. You would not see it till you walk up to it because the other trees are so full of dirty leaves.

Six weeks have gone by, and he comes to the last tree. The seventh one looks dead; it has only ten leaves on it now, and the bark looks bad, so dead looking. You can push the tree over. He cleans the tree using a ladder. He doesn't want to climb this dead tree. Cleaning the leaves quick, he does the digging around the roots and puts in new fertilizer and dirt. With all the trees cleaned and fertilizing is done, time will tell what nature does for all the trees. He buys two truckloads of wood chips and, with a wheelbarrow, spreads them over the backyard from the very back fence to the first of the orange trees. There is good grass that goes to the back of the nice-looking stepping-stones that he digs up, cleans, and straightens out at the back door of the house.

He's very busy with the shirts, working out, girls, and the house, and before he knows it, four months have passed quickly. He sees the trees are coved with the orange blossom flowers. He goes out back to smell the flowers on each tree. That fragrance puts you in heaven, but when he gets to the last tree, it looks dead; there is not one new leaf, but he gives the tree another week.

It's Friday late afternoon, and he goes out back to smell the orange blossoms. He smells each tree, and the fragrance is so fantastic it puts you in love land, especially when the flowers touch your face and you feel it so soft against your skin, plus the heavenly scent it gives. He walks up to the last tree and stands there just looking at the dead tree. The neighbor behind him north side, Miss Wilson, a very old lady, they have been talking off and on from the first day he moved into the house. She talks about her life, and he talks about Jesus and his life.

She comes out of one of the three houses that are on her property, saying, "Hello," and tells Freddy to cut that tree down and plant a new one. She is never short of words! She has witnessed all the other beauties unfold in his backyard, for she, too, works in her little green-house and vegetable garden.

He tells her, "I will first pray." He looks at the tree and then to the sky, then bows his head and says in his mind, *Father, this is your tree. Please do something. Thank you. Amen.* Miss Wilson walks away, and he goes back to the house. On Saturday morning, Freddy has lots to do and is gone the entire day. He comes home after dark and takes a shower with the Moody Blues playing in the background. Tired, he goes to bed and sleeps till just before dawn. Freddy has some store-bought orange juice. He's reads the Bible for an hour. It's after seven; it's Sunday morning. A thought pops into his head: *Let's go out to smell the orange blossom flowers.* He opens the back door and looks at the beautiful flowers covering all the trees, and he smells the beautiful fragrance in the air as he walks down the three steps over to the first tree on his right and walks around it. He is putting his face in the flowers, taking in a deep breath of loveliness. Watch out for the honeybees, the orange blossom fragrance is fantastic. He goes to the next, and the next, and the next; and when he gets to the last tree, the dead one, well! He sees that the whole tree is covered with green leaves, with full-grown oranges all over the tree. He steps back. He is blown away. This is jaw-dropping miracle, a dead tree on Friday evening, and now it has full-grown oranges to eat. He thanks God. What a fantastic miracle. This tree was dead, and now it is full of good-looking bell oranges and beautiful green leaves. *Did it happen overnight?* he thinks. *Does it matter?* He can't stop thanking the Father, Son, and Holy Spirit. He's being filled with extraordinary joy, and amazement.

Then Miss Wilson comes out of her house, and she looks at the tree, then at Freddy. She is not happy, and there is no smile on her face. Then she shakes her head. Then, without saying a word, she walks back into her house, and she does not know the joy of the Lord!

As he walks around the tree, there are no flowers, just oranges and leaves, all over this healthy-looking tree. He is so amazed at seeing this magnificent work of the Father. There is no doubt he created the earth in six days. Freddy steps back by ten feet, just to take it all in, with happiness in his heart.

Bill, the old man who walks around the neighborhood every morning and evening for ten years, has collected little toys that were thrown out in the trash. They are placed all around in his front and back yards. Bill and Freddy have talk for two years now. They live next to each other before Freddy bought the house. Now he's four houses away. It's funny that he comes over just after Miss Wilson walks into her house. He walks up to Freddy with his happy little smile, then looks at the tree. He then looks back at Freddy, his eyes wide open. He then turns and walks away very fast, shaking his head. Bill can't believe it. Just believe—that's all it takes. Freddy goes behind him, saying, "What do you think of God now!" Bill will not talk to Freddy. He just shakes his head, walking fast to the gate all the way to the front yard. On his way home, he feels afraid of something. Freddy says, "See what God can do!" Bill has seen the tree when it was dead. "Cut it down," he would tell Freddy. Freddy has told him many of times about Jesus and the Bible; Bill brushes it off as fairy tales. "For we have not followed cunningly devised fables, when we made known unto you the power and coming of our Lord Jesus Christ, but were eyewitnesses of his majesty" (2 Peter 1:16). "The fool has said in his heart, there is no God."

Freddy turns and looks at his backyard with the wooden gate open. The thought comes in like a wave: *If you tell the newspeople you will have people coming over to see the tree, maybe steal the oranges or the nuts that will come over to worship the tree, all kinds of people all the time day or night.* He walks back to the tree thanking God our Father and takes an orange and eats it. It is juicy good, and he picks enough to squeeze. Then he goes back to the house to make a glass of freshly squeezed orange juice. After a glass on ice, he makes the decision not to call the newspeople. He'll just tell a lost soul when the Holy Spirit moves him. "As the garden causes the things that are sown in it to spring forth, so the Lord God will cause righteousness, and praise to spring forth before all the nations. Some plant while others water or weed, but it is God who gives the increase" (Isaiah 61:11).

He has not told anyone in three months about the orange tree, and he has just gotten the newspaper and reads that Miss Wilson just died. Then another month goes by, and Bill dies. Freddy's witnesses are gone in four months after the miracle, but all the trees have oranges now, and he still has not told anyone about the miracle from the Father. He's just thankful for another fantastic miracle. Only three persons have seen the tree dead before the rebirth (but those two are dead) and Freddy. He keeps it to himself.

Life is good. The house is all painted in and out. The solid wood floors are sanded and restrained. All the oranges trees have oranges, and the shirts are selling like hotcakes. He is going to different churches each Sunday to hear the word of God from a mix of preachers. He does not want to be too close to anyone church right now. Variety is the spice of life. He is having fun with lots of women, but he knows this is not the right action for a man of God. He should have been letting the Holy Spirit guide him and setting a better example. He's running away from his calling. The Father has blessed him with so much. He is being selfish knowing all the Father has done for him but keeping it all to himself. He should be telling the world but does not want the negative that come with it. Silence is golden, but he still has lots of faith, just like Abraham and all the others in the Bible.

It's summer, and his daughters are with him for three weeks. The girls get to be baptized because they love their daddy, and they brought it up to him. This is their idea. It is a special joy for daddy to see his two beautiful daughters show Daddy their interbelief and doing it on an outward sign.

Another summer has gone by, and everything is going great, but Freddy has been thinking it would be nice to have a son before he gets too old. It's a selfish reason; it's to pass on his calling to the son. The seven thunders must be uttered, but he doesn't want to be known, he has kept this secret to himself for so many years, but he has never stopped witnessing to new people, about the love of Jesus the Christ of the Father. Plus, he has so many wonders and signs to share, with more to come.

The girls he has been dating do not have what he thinks would be good stasher for a son. Just a pretty face will not do, and she must be tall. So getting married to have a son the girl must be someone special; the Lord will set it up.

Coming up is a T-shirt convention in Orlando for three days and he is going. Last year, he went to the one in Atlanta, Georgia, which was fun. He took the train from Fort Lauderdale to Jacksonville. It was very relaxing to see the state of Florida in an unusual way. Then he rented a car and drove to Atlanta and met some interesting people, especially girls and one who suited his fancy. A fun time was had by all.

This T-shirt convention is closer to home, and he has friends in Orlando to spend time with, and he knows there will be lots of girls up there. Thursday night, he checks in to his hotel room and calls his friends. Friday is all business, getting to know about equipment and shirts dealers all day and night. Saturday morning is about getting back to the show, meet more people, and get some innovative ideas. Saturday night is party night, and the boys go out to the bars to dance, drink, and have some fun, remembering the good old days. Men are lustful creatures. He must get a hold of his thoughts, put them under control, and only through the Holy

Spirit can that be achieved. The Father of us all gives us free will, and you know what free will gets you? Sometimes on the wrong road of life, lost in a lost world! Mosses told the Israelites that the money they had made by working their trade could be spent on anything. "And thou shalt bestow that money for whatsoever thy soul lust after, for Oxen, or for sheep, or for wine, or for strong drink, or for whatsoever thy soul desires: and thou shall eat there before the Lord thy God, and thou shall rejoice, thou and thine household" (Deuteronomy 14:26). They had to live by the Ten Commandments, plus more man-made rules to live by or be stoned to death, and I do not mean by smoking pot ether.

The first club is a bore. They have one drink, then off they go to another club. The next one is filled with more men than girls. They turn around and they leave. The third club is a charm; there are more girls. Freddy walks around to see if he gets to make eye contact with one of the pretty ones. He sees one as she talks to her friends. He works his way over there and goes up to ask her if she would like to dance. She nods her head, and they go to the dance floor. The music is loud, so they do not talk much, but the eye contact is there. After a few fast dances, there is a slow dance, and as they dance, he whispers sweet nothings in her ear. They like each other very much, so after the slow dance, they get drinks and go somewhere less noisy. There is something special with her—tall, good looks. Turns out she and her friends are staying at a hotel in Daytona Beach. They came to Orlando to have fun, plus one of the girl's father is a wealthy doctor. He has a nice winter home in Orlando that they all drive to after drinking for hours. They do what all young lovers do. They talk for hours and find they have lots in common, and the most important is they both wanted a son. Then they enjoy being with each other till the sun comes up, and they walk outside and watch Mr. Sunrise.

Freddy likes everything about Suey-Q, and he knows she's the one he want to have his son with. She likes him as well and believes in having a son with him. The girls are going back to Daytona Beach, but they will call each other every night on the phone. They make plans to see each other in one month.

A month has gone by, and he flies up to Nashville. She picks him up at the airport, and they go to her apartment, and there they enjoy each other for the weekend.

On Monday, she has to go to work, and when she comes home, Freddy has made a tape with words and music of a marriage proposal, and he plays it for her. When it is over, he gives her a ring to show his love and devotion till death do they part. He knows this one will be able to stop his addiction with wanting to have sex with each pretty lady who comes into his world. The weekend is coming, and he is to meet her Mother. It was planned before he came up. Suey-Q didn't know he was going to propose, so she is very surprised and happy, for she wants to move to Florida and have a boy as well.

The day of the family gathering arrives, and he meets the nicest people anyone can get acquainted with. Her grandfather's house and farm was built back in the 1940s, and it was nicely built on over two hundred acres of land. Around his land are woods and other farmland. Kentucky is beautiful. America was built on good people like these. Her grandmother is a believer in Christ. She reads her Bible every day. She was very involved in the church, but it stopped there. The next generation rebelled and didn't go to church, and so it was with his new love. "Love is not blind that is the last thing it is, Love is bound and the more it is bound the less it is blind" (G. K. Chestertos).

All in God's timing, he knows all and sees all, and he will let it be known to you all if you paid attention to his voice the Holy Spirit.

Back at the apartment in Nashville, they lie together as one, just like the first day they met. It's so nice to be in love, but there is not a thing that can beat the Father's love. We are human, and our love is weak. God's love is all you need.

The next weekend, they go to see the King of Rock and Roll, his home, Graceland, where he is buried. Freddy knows he is with God, the Father of us all, for believers are forgiven of sin because of Christ Jesus, and he has a plan for this world. Freddy knows the Moody Blues and him are here for God's plan. He keeps this secret in his heart till the time is right; he knows he will be looked at as a nut, but if he says nothing, many souls will be lost. "Blessed is the man that trusteth in the Lord, and whose hope the Lord is."

"The heart is deceitful above all things, and desperately wicked: who can know it? I the Lord search the heart, I try the reins, even to give every man according to his ways, and according to the fruit of his doings" (Jeremiah 77:9–10).

He's back in Fort Lauderdale to work and getting things ready for his love to move down. Then in three months, Freddy flies up to Kentucky to pick up the woman who will have his son, his love. They rent a small trailer and hitch it to her car. She gives most of her things to her mother, and they pack up the rest and headed south. They leave at 3:00 a.m. very happy, in love with each other. An hour into the darkness on the drive, they see a bright shooting star; they turn their heads to look and makes eye contact at each other, and he says, "That was cool. We're having a son."

Two days later, they pull up to the house, and he gives her the tour of the inside walking in the front door is the living/small dining room the very small kitchen, bathroom, the bigger bedroom, and the art/ prayer room. To her, it's not so great, but she does not know all the work he put into this old home. Then the backyard, as they step out of the kitchen's back door down three steps onto a two-cement stepping stones that made up the four-by-eight-foot area, then onto grass, ten feet by twenty-five feet of nice green grass, then the wood chips covering the ground. He walks her up to the last tree and tells her the miracle of the orange tree that was dead and now is alive. A few weeks have gone by. She has gotten a job, and his T-shirt business is doing okay. They enjoy each other's company. Freddy is reading the Bible more now. In fact, every morning, he gets up an hour earlier to pray and read God's Word. He has one woman, and the love is growing, but she is complaining about his love for Jesus. After having the dead orange tree produce oranges and leaves in a day and a half, you would praise Jesus more because you know the Father's love is real. With the accident and many other signs and wonders, he can never stop thanking the Lord.

Seven months go by, and she is pregnant. They are both very excited. They work on the small bedroom, taking out his things, cleaning top to bottom, then putting the one-hundred-year-old rocking cradle that he was put in after he was born.

Another four months go by, and they drive up to Kentucky to see her mother and family to tell them the good news in person.

When they get back home, she quits her job, and payment of all the bills falls on his shoulders from then on.

They find out their baby will be a girl, and the mother is not happy. She wants a boy, and from that moment on, she is not happy anymore with Freddy. Another five months have passed, and he is standing in the delivery room with a camera when the beautiful girl has come into the world. He could not do this with his first two girls. In fact, when his first daughter was born, he had tickets to the first Moody Blues concert in Miami, but that night, he had to walk around the hospital, watching and waiting for a friend to play with. He was not expecting the joy that was coming his way. Now he knows how much love, joy, and fun children can be, bringing them up with the love of the Lord, for we are his children. Now he understands the parable of the prodigal son and how the oldest son could not understand how the father could forgive the son who took all his inheritance and spent it all foolishly and still love him because he was lost and then found. Without having children, it will be harder to know this kind of love the Father has for humans.

His third daughter is healthy and pretty, just like his first two. She grows fast and at the age of seven months, she walks like she knew what she was doing. Daddy takes her to every park in a ten-mile circumference of the house, for she likes to run, climb, but most of all swing. Daddy has a hammock between two of the oranges trees he put up after he cleaned all the trees. He would swing her and tell her story he makes up, mostly of animals that learned a very valuable lesson in life. On Saturdays, as she is growing up, he would watch the *Pee-wee Herman Show*, *The Anger Beavers*, and *The Rent & Stimpy Show* with her. Daddy would put on a puppet show whenever he has time any day of the week; he likes to see her laugh. The most important thing he shows her is how God loves us. "The most important thing a father can do for his children is to let them know about Jesus the Christ of God."

One morning, Freddy can't get out of bed. Everything on his left side is paralyzed. He can't move; the pain is really bad. On a scale of 1 to 5, it is a 10. He is taken to the hospital the next day, and his back doctor takes out his L5 disk that pops out and is pushing on the nerve. He is in the hospital for one week. When he gets home, he knows for sure he can keep the T-shirt shop, so he sold it at pennies on the dollar. After six months, God blesses him with a healing of the back and with a wonderful job two blocks from the house. He doesn't need the car to get to work. He just walks, so having one car is good for them.

Time keeps on ticking into the future, and another beautiful girl is born, and he has to work even harder, so Saturdays are workdays for him now, and soon Sundays will be also. When his fourth daughter is three years old, she asks her daddy when they are out front of the house playing and the sunset is a pretty sight, "When I was in my mommy's belly, was the sky as pretty as this?" He picks her up and gives her a hug, and he tells her, "I love you. What a great question. Yes, the sunsets are different each day, and some are as beautiful as this one."

He starts working seven days a week now to make ends meet, and after work on the days he can, he works on the home. Before he got married, he put together a shed in the far back corner of the backyard. Now from the shed door, he put in a wooden walkway that is four feet wide and forty feet long, and it ends where the concert slab will soon be. He's always up early to read his Bible. This is the twenty-seventh time he read through the sixty-six books, but it's time for a new Bible, and his wife gets one for his birthday. He puts a nice cover on it and starts transferring all his notes from his old Bible to the new one, and there is a lot.

A good year later, he built this slab that is sixteen feet by forty feet long, the length of the house. He does this by pouring two eighty-pound bags of cement into a wheelbarrow, mixing it up, then pouring it into the four feet by eight feet wooden frame he built with the steel wire mesh in the frame on the ground but lift it up after pouring in the cement. After the first pouring, then filling the next barrel, he does this so many times, so he knows that God is giving him the strength to do all this work. His good friend pulls the permit and helps him with putting in the 220-electrical line from the FPL poll in front by the road to the house. Freddy pulls the line that runs under the house for the washer and dryer and new stove. A lot of work is done in the house. He has to move the water heater three times because he pours only four feet by eight feet each night after work. When that is done, he then builds a canvas covering that shades the whole cement floor, and that can come down if a hurricane comes, but it is strong enough to stay up for a summer storm to keep things dry.

When the girls were very young, he built a tower, four feet wide by sixteen feet in height. The bunnies lived ground floors; there was a plastic pan under the cage that was pulled out to be cleaned two times a week of rabbit droppings. The second floor was a lookout station and a slide down to the sand area. The third was to see the top of the orange trees and of the neighborhood or the stars at night. The girls loved the hammock the best. They loved the swinging, and the stories Daddy would tell about animals that learned a lesson about life, God, and Jesus, and stories in the Bible. Finally, Freddy gets a promotion at work, so he stops working on Sundays to spend time with family.

The family is going to church on Saturday night at Calvary chapel. The church has moved from their first location to a bigger location, which they are going to the big beautiful place of fellow believers. When they first started going to church, Freddy got involved. On Saturdays, he would clean all the windows or help with any other project that need to be done. On Wednesday, he would teach the five- to seven-year-olds whatever the church had planned for them, and also play a game of football, the one you play with a flowed-up sheet of paper. You would play on top of the table, and they loved it. This is before the church moved into the big brand-new building, where they are now.

It's Wednesday around five in the afternoon, about an hour before going to church to spend time with the church kids. Freddy always took his Bible with the little book in the zipper cover that covered the Bible. That would go into a briefcase with papers that the children had done. Freddy is walking from the sofa to the bedroom. The voice comes to him loud and clear: "Your Bible is going to be stolen tonight!" He stops in his tracks; the Holy Spirit just spoke loud and clear. Without any hesitation, he takes out the little book and puts it in a safe place. He puts his Bible in the briefcase, thinking no one would steal a Bible. "Let's see if it gets stolen," he says. Then off he goes to church. When he gets to class, he puts his briefcase on top of the seven-foot filing cabinet. He has done this every Wednesday for over a year. He goes to the cafe to get a smoothie. They're finally getting popular now. He says hello to his friends and comes back to the classroom. Not long after, maybe ten or fifteen minutes tops, bingo, he guessed right; his briefcase is gone. His Bible is stolen. At that moment, he knows how important his Bible is, and he is saddened. His wife and daughters gave it to him. Plus he just finished putting in the information from his old Bible, but at the same time, he has a joy knowing the Holy Spirit has spoken to him again. He is so happy, that he put the little book in a safe place, to save the little book. He prays day and night for his Bible to be returned. He checks lost and found on Wednesdays and Saturdays nights, and he feels so sick he lost his Bible. On the third week, it's in the lost and found on Wednesday night service at church with the cover off and the Bible all wet. If he had not taken out the little book, it would have been lost forever. He takes the

Bible home and puts it in the microwave to dry it out, and then he irons every page to get out the wrinkles. He has not stopped thanking the Father since he found it. With his tears over and over, he cannot stop thanking God. When you are given a Bible and start reading it, you write on the side of pages about things the Holy Spirit has told you, or underline special words that have great meaning to you. You do not want to lose those special moments. The next day, he buys a new cover and puts it over his Bible, then the little book in the front zipper area of the new cover, and he thanks the Father over and over for saving the little book and his Bible. Somewhere over time, the book *Wisdom of the Spiritual Heart* goes missing.

# Chapter 7

## Seventh Sojourn

*"Isn't life strange a turn of the page, a book without lines unless with love we write?"*

The everyday life is the same, demanding work, church, and fun with the family. Years have gone by, and it's 1997. Freddy's up before sunrise on a Sunday morning, a habit he keeps up from being in the country club. He is reading the book of Revelations. He has read through the Bible thirty-two times from cover to cover, and the New Testament fifty times over. He is finishing chapter 9 going into 10, and after reading four verses, the Holy Spirit speaks to him, in the right side of the mind: "You know the seven thunders that must utter, and you have the little book." He put his Bible down; in a moment, in a twin-kling of an eye, everything the Father has done or said to him flashes through his mind, from when he heard the voice of the Father having his mind open, as a baby, his baptism at twelve, the bubble of love, the third eye, enlightenment walking to Daytona Beach, and on the seventh day being filled with love and truth about Christ. His fast and to know the seven thunders that will utter their voices. The marijuana rip-off, and being given the bullet, he is saved again, then going to the country club, and given the book *Wisdom of the Spiritual Heart*. His construction accident, how he was saved again, his hands pulled apart, then the push. The orange tree was an eye-opening experience, drop-dead, so in-your-face. Christ and his passion and resurrection, how the Father can do anything, how he has full control whether you believe or not. Your Bible will be stolen; the little book was put away in a save place, and here, now in the living room, sitting on the recliner. The Holy Spirit tells him what he has known for sixteen years, his secret, of who he is, the seventh angel, the messenger. He puts his Bible on the chair and walks around the living room, thanking the Father, Son, and Holy Spirit, then in the kitchen to drink some fresh squeeze orange juice from the Father's trees. He comes back to his chair, and he reads on in chapter 10. Then the Holy Spirit shows him in the scriptures that the seventh angel or messenger when he roars, lets out his voice.

"And the seventh angel sounded; and there were great voices in heaven, saying, the kingdoms of this world are become the kingdom of our Lord, and of his Christ; and he shall reign for ever and ever" (chapter 11:15).

"And the seventh angel poured out his vail into the air; and there came a great voice, out of the temple of heaven, from the throne, saying, it is done. And there were voices, and thunders, and lightnings; and there was a great earthquake, such as was not since men were upon the earth, so mighty an earthquake, and so great" (Revelation 16:17–18).

When the earth will shake, the Lamb's book of life will be closed. He reads through the book of Revelation to the end of the book how the New Jerusalem is coming down. It's a happy ending for believers. Every happy ending needs to have a start. Just open your heart, and let the Holy Spirit come in.

Have you started your walk with Christ Jesus yet? Freddy's life with Jesus has been a blessing. All he is, is a messenger; it's up to you to believe.

Freddy know, his calling is to roar as a lion to the unbelievers and believers, the ones who believe Jesus died for our sins and that he was God in the flesh on earth to the people of Israel, saying, "You are a prince of God, children of light on earth."

The Holy Spirit sends a strong impression in his mind "Now put in the air the seven thunders that must utter; on the radio, TV, and on the Internet the seven thunders that will utter their voices. The seven albums of the Moody Blues their walk was your walk to know Christ." "Yasha, Jesus the Christ of the Father who sent his Holy Spirit they are all one." Get to know this truth: the Holy Spirit leads you to Christ, Christ shows you the Father, and to become a child of light, "Living In God's Holy Thoughts." "This then is the message which we have heard of him, and declared unto you, that God is light; in him there is no darkness at all" (1 John 1:15).

He gets up and puts his Bible on top of the cabinet and walks out to the backyard, thanking the Father for everything. As he walks up to the miracle orange tree, it's still producing fruit. He's looking at it, should he have told the media when he had two witness he was thinking, Father *forgive me for being selfish.* Then he gets into the hammock and starts swinging. He thinks on what has just happened. His calling has come back. He must blow the trumpet. It's his calling. What the Father has asked him to do. This will not be easy. It will be hard to do. It will change his life, his family's life; everyone will think he has lost his mind. He's the seventh angel. He knows he is no angel, with the way he has lived, but he, too, forgets when God forgives, he remembers your sins no more, and his Holy Spirit is in you. That's what the Father sees. He knows your heart. He sees the Christ in you. It's not easy to give up on being human and letting the Holy Spirit take over your life. Paul put it this way in Romans 8,

There is therefore now no condemnation to them which are in Christ Jesus who walk not after the flesh, but after the Spirit. For the law of the Spirit of life in Christ Jesus has made me free from the law of sin and death. For what the law could not do, in that it was weak through the flash, God sending his own Son in the likeness of sinful flesh, and for sin, condemned sin in the flesh: That the righteousness of the law might be fulfilled in us, who walk not after the flesh, but after the Spirit. For they that are after the flesh do mind the things of the flesh; but they that are after the Spirit the things of the Spirit. For to be carnally minded is death; but to be spiritually minded is life and peace. Because the carnal mind is enmity against God: for it is not subject to the law of God Spirit, if so be that the Spirit of God dwell in you. Now if any man has not the Spirit of Christ, neither indeed can be. So, then they that are in the flesh cannot please God. But you are not in the flesh, but in the he is none of his. And if Christ be in you, the body is dead because of sin; but the Spirit is life because of righteousness. But if the Spirit of him that raised up Jesus from the dead dwell in you, he that raised up Christ from the dead shall also quicken your mortal bodies by his Spirit that dwelleth in you. Therefore, brethren, we are debtors, not to the flesh, to live after the flesh. For if we live after the flesh, you shall die: but if you through the Spirit do mortify the deeds of the body, you shall live. For as many as are led by the Spirit of God, they are the **Sons of God**. For you have not received the Spirit of bondage again to fear; but you have received the Spirit of adoption, whereby we cry, Abba, Father. The Spirit itself beareth witness with our spirit, that we are the Children of God.

(Please read the rest in your Bible).

He is still swinging when he asks the Holy Spirit when will the earth shake? As soon as he asks, these days pops into his mind: January 25 and 26. The world is either one of those days at the same time. There is no year. He gets not the year, so he only knows the days.

(Letting this book out now because it's God's timing, and it looks like the season is here.) As the hammock is slowing down, he thinks on how to set up the design on the Internet, the face shining as the Son. Days go by, and through the Holy Spirit, he is shown in the Bible that all believers are to be Israel, which means a prince of God. We will be living in his light. "For I am the Lord thy God, the Holy One of Israel, your savior:" "Even every one that is called by my name: for I have create him for my glory, I have formed him; yes, I have made him . . . I am the Lord, your Holy One, the creator of Israel your King" (Isaiah 43:3, 7, 15).

"That which we have seen and heard declare we unto you, that you also may have fellowship with us: and truly our fellowship is with the Father, and with his son Jesus Christ. And these things write we unto you, that your joy may be full. This then is the message which we have heard of him, and declare unto you, that God is light, and in him is no darkness at all. if we say we have fellowship with him, and walk in darkness, we lie, and do not the truth: But if we walk in the light, as he is in the light, we have fellowship one with another, and the blood of Jesus Christ his Son cleanseth us from all Sin" (1 John 1:3–7).

Living

In

Gods

Holy

Thoughts

Out of the book *Wisdom of the Spiritual Heart*

Psalm 118:27

"Whosoever follows me will never walk in darkness, but will have the light of life" (John 8:12).

For a month, he tells no one as he had with all his other mind-blowing miracles but starts to get everything on paper. On Sundays, he doesn't read his Bible for a spell. He just writes his story of all his miracles in his life and let the power of the Holy Spirit move him to put out what's going on the air.

Another year has gone by, and he has what he is going to put on www.seventhmessenger.com. He gets in touch with friends who help him get the websites going to put the Seventhmassenger. com out in the air. The next pages are what was put out on the Internet.

"Angels are spirits, but it is not because they are spirits that they are angels. They become Angels when they are sent. For the name Angel refers to their office, not their nature. You ask the name of this nature. It is spirit; you ask its office. It is that of an angel, which is a messenger" (St. Augustine, 354–430ce).

The word *angel* comes from ancient Greek word *angelos*, meaning "messenger." *Angelos* were the translation of a Hebrew word *mal-ak*, which also means "messenger." So as St. Thomas Aquinas pointed out in his great theological work *Summa Theologiae* (1266–1273), "We define, and can only define, angels by what they do, and not by what they are."

Angels are used by God to carry out the divine will, in great and small things alike.

They are messengers.

http://www.jpsc.net/7thmessenger/index.html

# Recommended Readings

Please read these chapters in the *King James Version of the Bible*.

Believers know this.

Revelation 10:1–11

Revelation 11:13–19

Revelation 16:17–21

Revelation 20:1–15

Before going on, thank you!

Hello, visitors,

First! The rainbow belongs to the Father. Everything does.

Do you ever get the feeling that it's all coming true?

The Bible you've been reading, is it really, really true?

Yes! We are in Revelation 10! I am the seventh angel, to let you believers know. We will become God's children, children in the Father's paradise.

The seventh messenger is only a believer's friend to tell God's children we're almost at the end.

Now you might not believe me with what I've been told to say! You will only know it's true!— when it happens, anyway.

So here is the message!

The seventh angel is told to say to believers and those who want to believe, across all nations.

Only by the Holy Spirit, whom the Father in the name of Christ Yeshua, Jesus, shall you learn all things (John 14:26).

The Holy Spirit has let it be known to me, the seven thunders that will utter their voices!

They will be put on this website.

I know the day! But I do not know the year.

I know it's the season, and the season is here!

The day the Father has given to me is in my heart of hearts waiting to be set free. "Yeshua, Jesus the true vine, the father is the husband-man, every branch in Christ that beareth not fruit, the Father taketh away: and every branch that beareth fruit, he purgeth it, that it may bring forth more fruit" (John 15:1–2).

"The Lord has made bare his Holy Arm in the eyes of all the nation; and all the ends of the earth shall see the salvation of our God" (Isaiah 52:10).

The God of Israel!

"Found everywhere in the Bible. God who at sundry times spoke in time past unto the fathers by the prophets. Hath in these last days spoken unto us by his Son, whom he has appointed heir of all things, by whom also he made the worlds" (Hebrews 1:1–3).

"They that has an ear, let them hear what the Spirit saith unto the body of believers, to them that over cometh will I give to eat of the tree of life, which is in the midst of the paradise of God" (Revelation 2:7).

This is a very simple message. I know it to be true only by the Holy Spirit, letting me know!

Asking me! To tell you! That there should be time no longer: It is done!

The Lamb's book of life (Revelation 13:8–9).

This book is soon to be closed! This book will have all the names of all believers in the Father's Christ. His name is Yeshua, Jesus!

You will know when the last name is added to the Lamb's book of life. A great earthquake will be felt around the world, and the whole earth will shake! Mediators will start hitting the earth, and the seas will rise around the world.

This is a marvelous eye-opening time. The age of computers, where this seventh messenger, message can be sent around the whole world in a blink of an eye.

Let's do the Father's will. By telling people about the Christ of the Father, Yeshua, Jesus.

You! Reading this message! Is your name written in that book?

The Lamb's book of life. The Father is giving you time right now!

Ask the Christ of God, Yeshua, Jesus, into your heart. Now is a good time! "Because of the

Lord that is faithful, and the Holy One of Israel, and he shall choose thee" (Isaiah 49:7).

When done with a true believing heart, the Father knows your heart. Your name is added to the Lamb's book of life.

"That the God of our Lord Jesus the Christ, the Father of Glory may give unto you the Spirit of wisdom and revelation in the knowledge of him: The eyes of your understanding being enlightened" (Ephesians 1:17–23).

The Holy Spirit comes inside of you to help you to know the truth, and the truth will set you free!

For spiritual fun, start loving your Bible!

"You who do not want Christ, you will be eliminated from this planet.

Let the sinners be consumed out of the earth, and let the wicked be no more. Bless thou the Lord, O my soul.

Praise you the Lord" (Psalm 104:35).

Only the children of light will live here on earth. Evil will be out of our hearts and mind. Talk about a beautiful world! Time is now to spread the word. Let Christ be your choice!

Because it's all coming true and it's all being witnessed now by *you*!

I hope you get the picture?

The Father has to step in and get the human on the right path.

There is only *one* Father, Son, and Holy Spirit. *One! All* are one.

My prayer is that you open your heart, and that's a start. Let your soul be written in the Lamb's book of life.

Before the earth starters shaken, not stirred.

Christ be within you.

Seventh messenger

FREDERICK F. HAUSSMAN JR.

Living

In

God's

Holy

Thoughts

If there be Christ in the heart, there will be beauty in the character.

If there be beauty in the character, there will be harmony in the home,

If there be harmony in the home, there will be order in the Nation.

If there is order in the Nation, there will be Peace in the world.

Please read these scriptures; Joshua 7:14, 1st Samuel16:7,Isaiah55:4-6-13&32:1,Roman's3:22-24, 1st John 4:14-21, Revelation 19:6-11 21:6-7

# Spiritual Heart

## Matthew 25:31–46

He gets in touch with people, but as what he thought would happen, they think he is nuts. So Freddy does nothing, and he knows when he cries with a loud voice as a lion roars, the media would be hounding him, family, and friends— all the headaches. Life is hard enough. Why make it harder? Just enjoy the Father's love. So he says, "If I do nothing, the earth will shake." He knows he is like Jonah, and the whale; he's running away from his calling. The Father can change his heart in a blink of an eye. Freddy has free will. His secret is his for now. He knows the Father of us all loves us. He will never leave you. Thank you, Father. The judgment day of us all is coming. You cannot stop it from coming. But you can make your afterlife better by accepting Yasha, Jesus the Christ of God.

Two years pass, and the family needs more space. The girls are getting bigger. They need their own rooms. So Freddy prays, "Should I sell the house, Father?" The next day, there is a real estate flyer on the door. In 1999, he sells the house, one of the blessings from the Lord. He moves to Port St. Lucie, another blessing. The house has a two-car garage. It's a 3/2, with a pool in the middle of almost a half acre of land.

Because of the travel time to work his hours are changed, so he is in bed by 8:30 up and out the door before 4:00 a.m. After years of working very hard at work and working around the new home and land, using a bucket truck, he cuts down five tall pine trees on his property. The pine needles kill the grass; plus racking up all the pine needles is a pain. After cutting the trees, that leads to always mowing the lawn and taking care of the pool, and he puts together a place to meditate and read his Bible. He calls it God's garden (Genesis 2:8–9, Revelation 2:7). With twelve stepping-stones, each stone represents one of the twelve tribes of Israel. They are going around the new orange tree, which he wanted to remind him of the orange tree God brought back to life, just like Christ's death and resurrection. That brings you to the Father of all creation. He puts in a nice two-seater swing where he would read his Bible in the mornings on weekends and in the early evenings after all work's done.

While at work, on one of his birthdays, in the fence that goes around the big yard, a turtle gets stuck. His girls hear all three dogs barking, and they want to check out the noise. It is that the turtle gets stuck in the fence. That evening, they give the turtle to their daddy in a wrapped box. Funny thing is, two weeks earlier, the girls ask their daddy what is his favorite animal. He says, "Turtle because they do not make any noise. You do not wash them or clean up their mess."

Now every Sunday morning, the turtle walks up to Freddy as he sits in the swing, and he hand-feeds the turtle with a peeled banana. The turtle would bite and swallow, then bite again until he is full, then walk away. He doesn't need any love or attention, but Freddy loves the little guy. That turtle is from the Father of us all, just to show Freddy he is here. It is funny how the simplest prayers are assured, God knows all. He wants you to know his Christ because his blood was shed for your sins!

Whenever God shines his light on
me and opens my eyes so I can see,

when I look up in the darkness night, I know everything will be all right. In deep confutation and great despair, when I reach out for him, he is there. When I'm lonely as I can be, I know God can shine his light on me. Reach out for him; he'll be there within, and you can share your troubles. If you live the life you love, you'll get the blessing from above. He heals the sick, and he heals the lame and says, "You can do it in Jesus's name." He lifts you up, and he turns you around. Then he puts your feet on higher ground (Van Morrison)

Then there was the ride to work each morning at 4:00 a.m., taking the turnpike, and two times the love of Christ, God's Holy Spirit fills him with his powerful love, just like in *Days of Future Past*, He tells Freddy, as this love is pouring into his heart, he can't stop crying. Feeling an unspeakable joy, he hears the Spirit say, "You're still my messenger." He has the website up but is doing very little about it. He just does not want the attention. Our heavenly Father fills him many times with his love, but Freddy tries to get it out of his thoughts to finish the book he started, to roar and tell all about the earthquake that is coming. He just wants to live a normal life with his family, no roaring like a lion. There is no doubt he is the seventh messenger; God has revealed it to him. He has a witness—the dead orange tree that came back to life. His wife does know about this special relationship he has had from birth with the Father of us all, but not yet his claim to be the seventh angel or messenger, to let the world know about the whole earth shaking violently.

Seven months has passed; vacation time is here, time for fun with the family and grandchildren, going to Disney World, good times had by all, making memories, staying in one of the delightful hotels on the property.

Time goes by to fast on vacation. They're back home and back to the routine of work and home schooling for the girls.

It's been three years of good times living in Port Saint Lucie. The year is 2003. One night, around 8:30 p.m. after looking at the TV for an hour, a thought pops into his mind before going to bed: *Go outside and see if the Father will send a shooting star*, and it was God that put the thought in his mind. He makes sure the outside light is off, and he goes out the front door and leaves it open. As he starts walking on the walkway beside the garage side wall, he lifts his eyes upward but quickly turns northeast. To his amazement, he sees what looks like, at first, a very big cruise ship in the sky, but it is way bigger! The floating condo does not have a pointed front nose. It's just floating in the air, very slowly going south. It's twelve stories high and longer than anything he has ever seen. Freddy is spooked as he is looking at this huge floating mothership for sure; he is thinking, *Is this the government spy ship, the NSA? What is this? How is this floating in the air without a sound?* As he stares at this huge something floating along, the voice in his right side in his ear says, "Guess how many souls live on this?" They are not persons; they are souls. He has heard this voice many times in his life. He is fifty-four, and this blows his mind on how God operates and where is heaven, now the mother ship it starts cloaking, and he can see the stars on the other side where the front is but still sees the big middle and the end. Thinking he might be beamed up because he is seeing this big floating mother ship, he sprints to the front door and into the house but then turns around and runs back. Maybe it takes three seconds, and it's gone—that fast. It was big, huge. he is blown way in all he believes, and he knows it's still floating. He just can't see it. There are only stars. He thinks we are definitely being observed, like being under a microscope, being scrutinized. This is bigger than his mind can understand, but he hears the voice say, "Guess how many souls live on this." What is this? Is it from God?

His mind hurts so bad, and he goes in the house and locks the door. He just goes in to bed. He must get up early for work. He tells no one about what he just saw, no one!—not even the dogs. He knows no one will believe him, but the dogs, who love without knowing when he tells them of this whatever it was the mother ship, and the voice they will just give him lots of love kisses as they are petted.

The Bible tells us, "Whosoever was not found written in the book of life was Cast into the lake of fire" (Revelation 20:15).

This is the second death. How sad it is that man rebels against God's Christ, Jesus, or Yasha?

A year has passed, and Freddy tears both medizes in his knees at work the year two hurricanes hit where they lived the first one was bad, no power for sixteen days, then another one, a month after getting power back on, back to back, just like his knees. The pain is in every step he takes. When he reaches his limit, he goes to workman comp. Then the wife decides to move back home. She misses her family and doesn't like the storms. Freddy loves Florida. He needs to have an operation on his knees, so they sell the house and go their ways. Freddy keeps in touch with the girls by calling every other day and driving up on visits after each operation on both knees. Freddy gets started on www.seventhmessenger.com again. He has moved in with his mother to help her and to heal after knees operations. He writes letters to tell his story first to Pastor James Kennedy, then Adrien Rogers. Both of them say, "You're nuts in a subtle way," but both of them die within months of each other. He has written to Oprah back in the '80s and other shows, and again 2005 with a letter to Billy Gram and others. He also talks to people at church and one of the writers of the book *Left Behind*. They all think he has lost it. He thinks that if the people of God do not care, then why waste his time? He keeps the website just sitting on the airwaves. He's not out to make money, but just get the word out to the people, unbelievers, and build believers' faith up in the Lord. Two years have gone by, and Freddy's knees are better, and he is sick of Fort Lauderdale; there are too many people, so he moves to Daytona Beach to hide and live there, trying not to roar. Everything is working out, and he is learning how to play golf.

Three years have passed, and in prayer one night, the Lord his Holy Spirit tells him he saw the New Jerusalem back in 2003, in Port Saint Lucie. He's so overwhelmed to hear that, and he thanks the Father, because he needed to know what that huge floating object was; that means it is of God's, but still he keeps it to himself. He reads in Revelations again, and it did look like what he read. "And the city lieth foursquare, and the length is as large as the breadth: and he measured the city with the reed, twelve thousand furlongs. The length and the breadth and the height of it are equal" (Revelation 21:16).

Freddy only saw the outside of this huge floating object. What John saw in Revelations 21:10–16 is more of the inside of the New Jerusalem.

He is working for five years now and living a good life, playing golf, walking to the beach, going to church services, and on Passover on the beach. The sunrise services are always beautiful, and he lets the seventh messenger website go off the air. His heart is hardened to do his calling for now. Just enjoy life, and golf game is getting better.

It's another two years, and Freddy is looking out the window on the seventh-floor apartment building. The view is nice, looking over the downtown toward the ocean. The rent is more, but the view is worth it. Then in his right ear, the Holy Spirit tells Freddy, "I have a better view for you!" It's been three years since the Spirit has told him about the New Jerusalem, and now a better view. Freddy does not take the apartment. He stays where he lives. He'll wait and see where the Father will send him. Another six months of working and playing golf has passed, and he has been calling his mother every other week for five years and going back down to Fort Lauderdale on her birthdays or Mother's Day to visit, but this time she has told him she needs to sell her house, and she needs his help to move. Two days pass by, and his brother in law needs a man to take care of his new building he bought, and he'll be the maintenance man. He needs to move back to Fort Lauderdale, and the view where he must live is beautiful. Just like what he heard, "I have a better view for you."

Let's bring Freddy's life on earth to this point of time 2017, all that the Father has shown him, his loving-kindness, his great miracle in 2003, the New Jerusalem he witnessed. He can't look away from it, but he is in fear to look at it. This New Jerusalem will come down when the Lord

Jesus will set up his kingdom on earth. Freddy does not know that day or time for that happing, the day of the Lord.

"For, behold, I create new heavens and a new earth: and the former shall not be remembered, nor come into mind. But be you glad and rejoice forever in that which I create: for, behold, I create Jerusalem a rejoicing, and her people a joy" (Isaiah 64:17–18).

Freddy does know that the earthquake is coming. All he knows is he must let it be known! So get your name in the Lamb's book of life, but it's funny how it's the Father that leads you to his Christ, and Christ leads you to the Father, but you must make the decision to ask and believe in Yasha, Jesus. Then his Holy Spirit comes into your heart and lives in you and helps you to be like Christ. You have free will, you make the call. If you have felt the Father calling you, say *yes* to his wishes and move to his light.

Come to the light, be children of light.

Living
In

God's
Holy
Thoughts

The earth will shake, and the lamb's book of life will closed! It's time to let you know! It's time for you to ask Jesus into your heart and mind, and believe he is the Christ of God, Lord of your life. Ask Yasha, Jesus, ask him to send his Holy Spirit to live in your heart and mind. Know and feel his love, grace, mercy, loving-kindness, for your soul to be at peace forever. For the earth will shake soon, and time is not on your side. A seventh-grader can figure this out—through the eyes of a child. Yes, you could live to be ninety-five and do good works, but to live for eternity is *oh*! so much better. So I have been given this time to finish my life story. Yes! In my story, the names have been changed to protect the innocent, but the truth be told your blood is not on my hands anymore! All of you have been worn. I have sounded the trumpet; I've done my part. This is what Jesus said to Paul, I pray to you, the reader:

"To open their eyes, and turn them from darkness to light, and from the power of Satan unto God, that they may receive forgiveness of sin, and inheritance among them which are sanctified by faith that is in me" (Jesus, Acts 26:18).

We are Israel, a prince of God, so if you have Jesus, you are in the family of Israel, the people of God's kingdom to come, his will be done, on earth as is in heaven.

"Know you therefore that they which are of faith, the same are the children of Abraham. And the scripture, foreseeing that God would justify the heathen through faith, preached before the gospel unto Abraham, saying, In the shall all nations be blessed. So, then they which be of faith are blessed with Faithful Abraham" (Galatians 3:7–9).

"The just shall live by faith. And the law is not of faith: but, the man that does them shall live by them. Christ has redeemed us from the curse of the law, being made a curse for us: for it is written, cursed is every one that hanged on a tree: That the blessing of Abraham might come on the gentiles through Christ; that we might receive the promise of the Spirit through faith" (Galatians 3:11–14).

"Now to Abraham and his seed were the promises made. He said not, and to seeds, as of many, but as one, and to thy seed, which is Christ" (Galatians 16).

"But the scripture has concluded all under sin, that the promise by faith of Jesus The Christ might be given to them that believe. But before faith came, we were kept under the law, shut up unto the faith which should afterwards be revealed. Wherefore the law was our schoolmaster to bring us unto Christ, that we might be justified by faith. But after that faith is come, we are no longer under the schoolmaster. For you are all children of God by faith in Christ Jesus. For as many as you have been baptized into Christ have put on Christ. There is neither Jew nor Greek, there is neither bond nor free, there is neither male nor female: for you are all one in Christ Jesus, and if you be Christ's then are you Abraham's seed, and heirs according to the promise" (Galatians 3: 7–29).

Therefore, we are all Israel that believe in Yasha, Jesus.

"And without controversy great is the mystery of godliness: God was manifest in the flesh, justified in the Spirit, seen of angels, preached unto the Gentiles, believed on in the world, received up to glory" (1 Timothy 3:16).

"Now the God of hope fill you with all joy, and peace in believing, that you may abound in hope, through the power of the Holy Spirit" (Romans 15:13).

"The Father has not given us the Spirit of fear; but the power, and of love, and of a sound mind. Be not thou therefore ashamed of the testimony of our Lord, nor of me his prisoner: but be thou partaker of the afflictions of the gospel according to the power of God; who has saved us, and called us with an Holy calling, not according to our works, but according to his own purpose and grace, which was given us in Christ Jesus before the world began, but now made manifest by the appearing of our Savior Jesus Christ, who has abolished death, and has brought life and immortality to light through the gospel: where

I am anointed a preacher, and an apostle, and a teacher of the Gentiles. For the which cause, I also suffer these things: nevertheless, I am not ashamed: for I know whom I have believed, and am persuaded that he is able to keep that which I have committed unto him against that day. Hold fast the form of sound words, which you have heard of me, in faith and love which is in Christ Jesus. That good thing which was committed unto thee keep by the Holy Spirit which dwells in us" (2 Timothy 1:7–14).

"I love in the truth; not I only, but also all they that have known the truth: For the truth sake, which dwelleth in us, and shall be with us forever. Grace be with you, mercy, and peace, from God the Father, and from the Lord Jesus Christ, the Christ of the Father, in truth and love."

See you on the other side of the shaking; believers in the Christ of God, Yasha, Jesus. "And I saw a new heaven and a new earth: for the first heaven and the first earth were passed away: and there was no more sea. And I John saw the holy city, new Jerusalem, coming down from God out of heaven, prepared as a bride adorned for her husband. And I heard a great voice out of heaven saying, Behold, the tabernacle of God is with men, and he will dwell with them, and they shall be his people. God himself shall be them and be their God" (Revelation 21:1–3).

"Yet the numbers of the children of Israel shall be as the sand of the sea, which cannot be measured nor numbered; and it shall come to pass, that in the place where it was said unto them, you are not my people, there it shall be said unto them, you are the sons of the living God. Then shall the children of Judah (the Jews) and the children of Israel (the believers in Christ Jesus) be gathered together, and appoint themselves one head, and they shall come up out of the land: for great shall be the day of Jezreel." Much more on this in Hosea 1:10–11.

Freddy a messenger from the Father, Son, and Holy Spirit to all the people on earth, "that there should be time no longer" (Revelation 10:1–11).

The seven thunders have uttered their voices! The seven albums of the Moody Blues—*Days of Future Past, In Search of the Lost Cord, To Our Children's Children's Children, On a Threshold of a Dream, Every Good Boy Deserves Favor*, *Question of Balance*, and the *Seventh Sojourn*— are the voices that must utter. If you have ears to hear, they will lead you to the Father and his Christ. The Father's music is the vibration of his love all around us. Open your heart. That's the start. Open your mind to a beautiful love relationship with the Father, Yasha, Jesus the Christ, and his Holy Spirit.

"The Ten Commandments, there they be, as the Lord commanded me. And now, Israel, what does the Lord thy God require thee, but to fear the Lord thy God, to walk in all his ways, and to love him, and to serve the Lord with all thy heart and with all thy soul, to keep the commandments of the Lord, and his statutes, which I command thee this day for your good? Behold, the heaven and the heaven of heavens is the Lord's thy God, the earth also, with all that therein is. Only the Lord had a delight in your fathers to love them, and he chose their seed after them, even you above all people, as it is this day. Circumcise therefore the foreshin of your heart, and be no more Stiff necked" (Deuteronomy 10:4-5, 12–16).

(Believers in God's Christ, Yasha, Jesus, and the Holy Spirit. We are his people Israel! (Israel meaning a Prince of God!) (Genesis 32:28).

Thank God for his grace and mercy, and we just have to believe Christ died for our sins.

True believers in Christ, the Father has your back, and you know that.

"It's all coming true, and it's all
being witnessed now, by you!"
Justin Hayward Songwriter

Love you all with the love of Christ.
Happy, Happy (Proverbs 16:20)
Joy, Joy (1st Peter 1:8)
Freddy
Brother in Christ Jesus

CPSIA information can be obtained
at www.ICGtesting.com
Printed in the USA
BVHW020617190719
553898BV00004B/20/P